Leave Only Footprints

A collection of columns
by A. C. Snow

Raleigh, N.C.

Cover photo by Walter D. Phillips
Cover design by Kate Newton Anthony

Special thanks to Pam Nelson, Angela Randolph and
The News & Observer production department.

Copyright 1994 by The News and Observer Publishing Co.
Library of Congress Catalog Number 94-068872

ISBN 0-935400-19-2

Also by A.C. Snow

Dust of Snow

Snow Flurries

Comfort Me With Apples

For my sisters, Zetta Snow Haynes and Ima Snow Paulson, whose affection and support in my youth influenced the course of my life, and for Katherine Weant Hill Brown, my wife's mother, in admiration of her courageous life and in gratitude for the fine qualities she instilled in her daughter, Nancy Jean.

Rich beyond belief

Wouldn't you think that the best and easiest part of birthing a book would be choosing its title? That's not always the case.

Well before the first book of Sno' Foolin' columns appeared in 1980, I knew that it would be named "Dust of Snow," the title of a short Robert Frost poem.

In my mind, a book's title should reflect something of the writer's personality, as well as a hint of the content. It should, of course, also command the attention of people browsing through bookstores.

"Snow Flurries," the title for the second collection, never really caught my fancy. But when I came across the phrase "Comfort Me With Apples," while leafing through Song of Solomon in The Bible during a Sunday morning church service, I knew I had a title I could like.

During the search for this book's title, a friend related an anecdote involving a famous writer on a lecture tour. It seemed that in every audience he addressed, there was someone who was in the process of writing a book and wanted advice on selecting its title.

One night, a particularly persistent would-be novelist kept asking the lecturer to suggest a title for her unpublished work.

"Madam, are there any bugles in your book?" the author asked.

Told there were no bugles, he then asked, "Are there any drums in your book?"

"Not one," the woman replied.

"Well then, Madam, why not title your book 'No Drums, No Bugles?'" said the exasperated author.

Several title suggestions were discarded for various reasons before that summer morning I took a stroll along the quiet strand at Indian Beach and came upon an anti-littering sign that said simply: "Leave Only Footprints."

Eureka!

After all, when life is over and done with, the most important things any of us leave behind are, as Longfellow said, "footprints on the sands of time."

We leave "footprints" on the children we have raised, the friends we have made, the students we have taught, the patients we have doctored, and, in the case of writers, on the people who have read what they have written.

It may be that the thousands of columns I have written over the long haul are footprints of a sort. True, most have been erased by the tide of time, but it may be that some of the "footprints" gathered in this volume will linger a little longer.

I am a very fortunate man. As followers of my column, published in The News and Observer and the Raleigh Times during the past 36 years, you have made my job the most enjoyable possible.

I once was autographing books in a Cameron Village bookstore when two boys, 10 or 11 years old, breezed past. Suddenly they stopped, backed up and looked at the book I was signing.

"You write that book?" asked an open-faced lad with piercing black eyes.

"Yes," I answered modestly.

"All right!" he exclaimed, admiringly, as if I had just scored a touchdown.

"Are you rich?" he asked.

"No way, fellow," I laughed.

But as the two went out the door, dark-eyes said to his friend, "Probably a billionaire!"

I still smile to myself at such a preposterous idea. Yet when I think about the years of pleasure I've received from writing, and the fact that someone turns to my place in the newspaper or goes into a bookstore and plunks down good money for something I have written, I have second thoughts.

I feel rich beyond belief.

—*A.C. Snow*

Contents

Tears of little boys of summer........1
Sleepless at 39,000 feet up!........3
He gives enemas to elephants........5
Encounter with a cold chicken........7
Living with a man's uniqueness........9
You don't have to lay an egg........11
Saying 'I'm sorry' isn't easy........13
Showdown with 'Cool Hand'........15
Back to the cliffs of Dover........17
Fathers in a field of dreams........19
Finally, the fat lady sang........21
Bad dogs in Paradise........23
Trouble with a capital 'T'........25
A bodice ripper to remember........27
Donaldson didn't do Fairmont........29
Why not just say 'fish?'........31
Dads don't always know best........33
Judged by the way we speak........35
'This is something I raised'........37
Why not call me 'Mister?'........39
He has meat in his suitcase........41
You go there; she takes you in........43
Living with LBJ a class act........45
And oh, it gave a lovely light........47
Guilt on the back of the bus........49
She has 'painful gas'........51
'Streaking' without style........53
Saving safety pins and past........55
Preachers' kids hurt, too........57
When 'angels' tinkle on stage........59
The nuttiest day of the year........61
So, what's a honeymoon?........63
A different hen each time........65
On the sad side of lonesome........67
Saluting 'Big Pilot in the Sky'........69
'Potatoe' no small potato........71
They're always 'only 18'........73
In every frog a handsome prince........75
God cranks a lawnmower........77

Forgiving Pearl Harbor..79
A bit of majesty in us all..81
Our Dolly had good position...83
Going on the pill..85
We are our brother's keeper..87
As useless as peacocks..89
Pawn shops don't sell myrrh...91
Kilroy was always there...93
Falling out of love raggedly..95
Revisiting old foxholes..97
Executioners can be gentle, too...99
One sour note, you're out..101
President Clinton's $4 skivvies..103
A best seller with spaghetti...105
Spend it all for loveliness..107
'Don't tell God I'm drunk!'..109
A common man's kind of car...111
Don't forget when they hugged..113
Bored stiff in Billings, Montana...115
Much ado over aviation and sex..117
Leave love letters in the sand..119
Adding up our great mistakes...121
Choosing our sons-in-law..123
Billy Graham: wine or water?...125
It won't happen on a Monday!..127
Seeking honest 4th graders..129
A wife with 50 pairs of shoes...131
A Madison County ending..133
God doesn't play basketball..135
Watching the liver bleed..137
The dean spins in her grave..139
Killing doesn't make a man..141
Two-minute eggs and speeches..143
If Mama ain't happy..145
Catching last bus to Heaven..147
'You're not listening, dear'..149
Fish more, make love less..151
Wee lads with 'girl problems'..153
A wench in good condition..155
What men want from life..157
When boyfriends won't sleep over..159
The heart's keen anguish...161

Quarterbacks cry when hit	*163*
Ode to a first violinist	*165*
Losing virginity worth a page	*167*
Sin, serendipity in the foothills	*169*
A hero without magic	*171*
There's joy in feeling guilty	*173*
Lacking the killer instinct	*175*
Tell the girl in Tony's room	*177*
It's never 'only a game'	*179*
Velvet I would wish her	*181*
The melodies linger on	*183*
Rare moments when men cry	*185*
It beats priming tobacco	*187*
Mozart in Wolfpack's den	*189*
Times's little ticking moments	*191*
Toast coach's 'lovely wife'	*193*
The right to remain naked	*195*
Four drinks, you're a pig	*197*
Going home	*199*

Tears of little boys of summer

On my evening walks, I pass the little boys of summer busy at the business of baseball at the elementary school ballpark near our house.

Their shrill, high-pitched voices echo across the field as a youngster smacks a single down to left field or slides in to score amid a cloud of dust.

Sometimes, there seem to be more parents than players on the field, egging on their offspring.

I cannot help it. I quickly search out the faces on the bench, faces that belong to the little guys who, as bench warmers, seldom get into the game. I've been there. I was a bench warmer.

At lunch recently, I asked the fellow across the table what kind of year his wife, an elementary school teacher, had experienced.

"Not the greatest," he smiled. "She's had an unusually rowdy crowd of youngsters this year. What's worse, she's had to contend with several rowdy parents. You know how it is. Parents are inclined to tell the teacher how to run her classroom."

"I know just how she feels," said another man at the table. "It was the parents who drove me out of coaching."

"Yeah," he said, in response to my questioning look. "At one time I coached Peewee baseball."

"I went into it with the idealistic idea that every kid would play. Equal time, regardless of talent. That even included Tommy, who couldn't hit a freight train headed for home plate or catch the moon if it were falling in the outfield."

"When we were stomped four games in a row, and the kids' parents were all over my back, I decided to be more selective. I played only the best players."

"Then I got a letter from Tommy's father, a professor at N.C. State, who wanted to know why Tommy wasn't playing, and particularly why my own son was permanently ensconced at first base."

"I told him, I was sorry, but winning is the bottom line. And realizing that, I gave up coaching."

There are two sides to this coin: the parents' side, the youngsters' side.

Chicago Times columnist Bob Greene some years ago described how a 9-year-old Little Leaguer named Brett suited up night after night, hoping to get in the game.

He practiced early and often, persuading his non-athletic Dad to go out in the yard to throw to him in order to "limber up."

Greene described how the boy would put on his uniform at home four hours before the game and walk around the house, looking at himself in the mirror. He would arrive at the field a quarter to five, just to be sure to be on time. Every game was going to be the one in which he'd finally play.

And his mother attended every game.

"Even from a distance, she would see those eyes lighting up every time he thought he might get to go in, and then she would see the coach not even knowing her son was there," Greene wrote.

She once asked him why, and the coach replied, "I have to keep the best ones in. We're in a league you know."

"One evening it happened: For some reason a lot of the boys had other things to do and there were only nine present when it was time for the game to begin. His mother was there again, and she saw the coach tell Brett that he was to start the game in right field.

"In the middle of the first inning, one of the regulars rode up on his bike. The coach was clearly glad to see him. When Brett trotted off the field, he saw the other boy had arrived. The coach took Brett out; his evening was over.

"The season is almost finished now. Brett does not put his uniform on four hours early anymore; he does not watch the clock. He still goes to the games but he has learned his lesson. He doesn't talk about baseball around the house."

That was the end of baseball for Brett, as it is for hundreds of kids like him. It hurts when you realize you aren't good enough, and that winning is what counts, not how you played the game. Or that you even play.

But you have to be a parent or the caretaker of a child to know this kind of special suffering.

You try to tell yourself and your child that maybe it's better to face up to reality, to realize early on that life isn't even or fair, that we are not all created equal when it comes to abilities, talents or whatever.

But I think that being chosen last, or not chosen at all, be it in love, baseball or a number of other things, goes a long way toward killing dreams.

And if a kid, or anyone for that matter, doesn't have a dream, what is there to life?

I would be a lousy coach. I would play them all and go home with the "Most Games Lost" award. And not be a bit ashamed of it.

May 1993

Sleepless at 39,000 feet up!

It is 2 a.m. by my watch as I write this on a plane plunging through the night between Raleigh-Durham and London's Gatwick Airport. I keep asking myself, "What am I doing here?"

If God had wanted man to fly at 39,000 feet above sea level, he would have cured man's fear of flying, which, according to surveys, ranks as one of man's five worst fears.

How can all these other passengers sprawled about me in various positions of sleep close their consciousness to the terrible things that can happen when you are suspended in space and darkness high above the ocean like this? Is their faith so great and mine so much less than a mustard seed?

Even my wife dozes fitfully beside me. Somebody has to stay awake to hold this thing up, if not physically, at least prayerfully.

I have flown, off and on, since I was an 18-year-old in the Air Force. But the feeling of being out of place so far above the earth is always with me.

I paid scant attention to those careful demonstrations on how to use the oxygen mask and "flotation" piece under my seat. I haven't even checked to see if it's there.

As unmechanical as I am, I'd probably blow up the "flotation" piece and strap the oxygen mask around my waist. Anyway, I'm enough of a realist to know what my chances are in the event of a crash.

If we go down, I will spend my last moments asking forgiveness for some things I have done and for others I haven't done.

It is now 2:30. The time drags. I have returned to "The Shipping News," Annie Proulx's Pulitzer Prize-winning novel my friend Shirley Hayes gave me to read on the crossing.

I feel like the hero's aunt who, during a terrifying two-day storm on the Newfoundland coast, is confined to a dingy motel room with her nephew and his two small children. She reacts like most of us caught in a tight spot.

"...If I ever get out of this motel I will lead a good life, go to church regularly, bake bread twice a week and never let the dirty dishes stand. I'll never go out with my legs bare, so help me, just let me get out of here."

I try to reassure myself. Very few planes crash. And the fact that before leaving home I paid only $10 for $300,000 worth of life insurance must mean something. I return to my book.

The night finally gave way to dawn. Breakfast was served. An hour later the the great bird glided gently down into Gatwick Airport. My heart leaped with relief. Anticipation of taking on the Brits soared at each bounce of the tires.

But during the 15 warm, almost rain-free days in the kingdom by the sea, my mind was never completely free of the haunting realization that I would have to do it all over again.

Airborne and headed home, I wonder about the guy up there in the cockpit responsible for the 170 lives aboard. What manner of man commands this monstrous ship that costs $60 million and defies gravity and imagination by lifting a weight of 340,000 pounds off the earth?

I keep remembering a long ago Lewis Grizzard column in which he wrote about a pilot who, just before departing for the Atlanta airport, had a bitter fight with his girlfriend.

Taxiing out to the runway for take-off, he suffered a temper tantrum and deliberately jammed his aircraft into another plane parked nearby.

"What can you tell me about our pilot? Is he married? Settled? Kids? Even-tempered?" I asked Janie Miller, our attractive and efficient young flight attendant.

She said she knew little about him, since she was subbing on this particular flight.

Shortly thereafter, Capt. Tom Castle himself appeared at our seats, knelt in the aisle and chatted amiably for a few moments.

A clean-cut likable bachelor from Seattle, he is the son of a World War II pilot and has had plenty of flying experience. I could only hope he had his love life well under control.

A mere mortal, "boy-next-door" type, he seemed as much at ease with his awesome job as plumbers, lawyers and newspaper columnists are with theirs.

When he is not piloting the American Airlines Boeing 767-200ER (extended range) to and fro across the big pond, he spends a great deal of time fishing and working with wood.

To those of you who suffer through similar anxiety attacks the moment you board a plane, I pass on a truth shared by a fellow in Edinburgh, Scotland.

"Statistics show that each year more people are kicked to death by donkeys than die in airplane crashes," he said.

So, go ahead, relax. Fly the friendly skies. But stay out of the way of donkeys. And when you arrive home safely, bake bread.

August 1994

He gives enemas to elephants

I read an article in the Wall Street Journal not long ago about people who in the Indian summer of their lives changed their whole outlook as well as their professions.

A man named Henry Felt did this. At age 50, he walked away from his job as a political analyst with the CIA. He crowded his wife and two daughters into a mobile home and became the manager of a small traveling circus.

From boyhood, he had always wanted to join the circus. When his doctor told him he had a year to live, he knew it was then or never. Now, 13 years later, he is really living — doing what he always wanted to do.

When I read the article, I remembered the story about a kid who ran away from home and followed the circus out of town.

When the circus returned to the same town a year or so later, two of the boy's buddies went out to visit him under the Big Top.

When they asked what he did with the circus, he said proudly, "I give enemas to elephants."

His pals were horrified.

"Benny," they said, "That's horrible. You must be kidding! You gotta ditch this job, right now!"

"And give up show business? No way," replied Benny.

I was one of those few boys who never had the urge to follow the elephants.

But as a farm boy watching the train rumbling by along the river as we worked the bottom land corn, I longed to be aboard and let it take me wherever it was going.

There is a restlessness about trains that touches the soul.

A 45-year-old friend of mine recently chucked his job as an educator to go back to law school. Another friend dreams of taking a year's leave from his well-established position to drive an 18-wheeler across the country.

And an orthopedic surgeon I know can't wait to retire from setting broken arms and replacing worn-out hips so he can spend full time repairing sick automobiles.

The nature of our jobs has a lot to do with our wanderlust or discontent. Growing up near Winston-Salem, I occasionally took the tour through the Camel cigarette factory there.

As young as I was, I was touched, even then, by the terrible monotony of an assembly line job. I studied the expressionless faces of the workers, mostly women, whose hands automatically played the endless stream of cigarette packs, scooping up 10 at a time and stuffing them into cartons. And I was frightened by the possibility of such a fate for me.

I also remember the little risque joke inspired by the brown and gold cigarette pack with the camel and pyramids on the front.

"Where is the man on a pack of Camels?" one of my little friends would ask.

"There is none," I would reply innocently.

"Oh, yes, there is. He has gone to pee behind the pyramids."

Camels or elephants, there is a bit of show business in all of us, and if our work does not provide a stage on which we can strut a little, life becomes colorless, purposeless. And sometimes intolerable.

One day I watched the operator of a big earth mover at the site of the new Wake County Jail skillfully maneuver the huge, snaggle-toothed scoop, as it took big bites of earth and spit them into waiting dump trucks.

He caught me watching, waved and did a couple of fancy flourishes with the awkward-looking scoop.

On another day I saw a window washer working his way up the face of a high-rise office building downtown. Several bystanders stood around on the sidewalk below, craning their necks, admiring his courage.

As the man maneuvered himself up to the next floor, a covey of pretty office girls rushed over to the glass wall, smiled and applauded.

Even a farmer, whose audience may consist only of a flock of crows as he tills his land and tries to outwit nature, strives for that precious high of accomplishment.

He becomes somebody with a capital S when at the country store he mentions that he has grown a 40-pound watermelon or that his second primings brought $175 a hundred this year.

As long as our jobs in some way make us feel important, give us identity and keep us off the assembly line, we will not run away to join the circus. Or look for the man behind the pyramid.

But if and when the light goes out of the task, any one of us may feel compelled to flutter our wings in a new direction. Many may take flight against the prevailing wind.

January 1990

Encounter with a cold chicken

I have a message today for the parents of boys. It's "Get 'em in the kitchen, early!"

Forget the foolishness about how real men don't eat quiche or cook. I was reared a victim of such nonsense. God has a way of punishing a man of that ilk. He lets his wife catch the flu.

Suddenly, the husband finds himself in the kitchen with no more idea of what's going on than a shade-tree mechanic trying to overhaul Voyager II an hour before liftoff.

When I arrived home from the office recently, I heard the sound of deep, rasping coughs from the back bedroom and realized I was in trouble.

On the kitchen counter, a sassy-looking chicken sat provocatively in a bowl of cold water, belly up, as if waiting for its tummy to be scratched.

As I walked into the bedroom, the patient raised her weary head and whispered hoarsely, "You might try to bake the chicken so Alean will have something for lunch tomorrow."

Alean is the wonderful woman who has been coming to our house every Wednesday for 28 years.

And for 28 years, the people at our house have hit the floor running every Wednesday morning "getting ready for Alean."

"Mama, if Alean's coming, why are we working so hard to get ready for her?" the children used to complain.

We all knew the answer. We loved Alean so much we wanted her approval on the condition of the house when she got there. So, I decided that, for Alean, but for nobody else, I would tackle the creepy-looking chicken.

My wife already had briefed me on the procedure weeks ago. In fact, she had written the instructions on a file card and left it out for me.

I was to reach into the hole in the chicken's fuselage and remove its "private parts," as I called them — the gizzard, neck, etc.

To me, this was the most repulsive part — an incredible, demeaning invasion of the chicken's privacy and my own delicate sensibilities.

I shut my eyes and groped for the hole. It wouldn't yield. I pulled. I pushed. The chicken resisted stubbornly.

Maybe I have the wrong end, I thought, and turned the chicken around. No entrance there. I returned to the other end and tried again. No luck.

How could I get the chicken to relax? I was in no mood to sweet-talk a dead bird. Not even for Alean.

Fortunately, I had bought a rib-eye steak on the way home. I muttered a few uncomplimentary remarks over the arrogant chicken, pushed her to the back of the kitchen counter and set about broiling the steak.

I was doing fine — even after extinguishing a couple of small grease fires — until the telephone rang.

How do they know? These cemetery lot salesmen who only call when someone in the house is running a fever of 102 degrees? I had the cemetery salesman to thank for a steak medium well rather than pleasantly pink.

Later in the evening, my wife dragged herself into the kitchen and deftly removed the package of discard from the chicken's interior.

"What did I do wrong?" I asked, describing my standoff with the chicken.

"Nothing. I guess it just hadn't thawed enough," she sighed. From there on, I was OK. I managed to bathe the bird inside and out, insert the spices into the cavity and tuck in the chicken's wings "so it will look pretty."

I even massaged the entire body with cooking oil and sprinkled it with paprika before shoving it into the oven.

When, an hour and a half later, I lifted the cover from the baking dish, I beheld a thing of beauty, golden brown, simmering in its own juices, sending forth a tantalizing aroma.

I was overcome by emotion. Uncanny as it seems, the thought of my first chicken brought to mind the lines from Browning's "My Last Duchess:"

That's my last Duchess painted on the wall.
Looking as if she were alive.

There was my first chicken sitting there, looking like a color photo from a Better Homes and Garden cookbook.

What I experienced with the chicken was the exhilaration we all feel when we have crossed over the barrier between ignorance and knowledge — whether it's not falling off the bike for the first time, scoring the first touchdown, changing the spark plugs in the car or kissing your first girlfriend.

It's the sweet smell of success, no matter how small. My whole life has new meaning. I have gone from a nothing in the kitchen to a cook.

Move over, Julia Child!

March 1993

Living with a man's 'uniqueness'

Another wedding. This time it was Sam Johnson's boy, Bill, two doors down the street. It's amazing how kids grow so tall in such a short time.

The bride was lovely, the groom handsome enough. I settled back to drowse through the wedding vows I must have heard a thousand times.

My ears perked up! What's this?

The minister, the Rev. Sandy McGeachy, former pastor of West Raleigh Presbyterian Church, was saying something different, something that made a lot of sense.

"Hold on to each other on the road of life," he advised the couple. "But do not get lost in each other. Discover all you can as a self and then share it with the other.

"In your togetherness, never lose your God-given uniqueness. Only as you are a separate person can you be a complete partner."

Ah, there's the rub. So many spouses find it difficult to live with each other's "uniqueness" and want to redesign their mates.

My wife's book club is reading Phyllis Rose's "Parallel Lives," the account of five Victorian marriages. Browsing through the book, I came across the very thing that Mr. McGeachy spoke of.

John Ruskin, English essayist and critic, immediately becomes disenchanted with his bride Effie:

"I married her thinking her so young and affectionate that I might influence her as I chose, and make of her just such a wife as I wanted," he wrote.

"It appeared that she married me thinking she could make of me just the husband she wanted. I was grieved and disappointed at finding I could not change her, and she was humiliated and irritated at finding she could not change me."

This is the same man who earlier had written Effie: "You are like a sweet forest of pleasant glades and whispering branches. ... You are like the bright — soft — swelling — lovely fields of a high glacier covered with fresh morning snow."

The marriage was never consummated. Five years later, Effie had it annulled and married one of Mr. Ruskin's good friends, painter John Everett Millais.

So there is good reason for me to peruse with great admiration those photos in Sunday pages of couples celebrating their 50th anniversaries. Undoubtedly for them there was considerable give and take before settling in for the long run and deciding that they couldn't or wouldn't try to change each other.

Undoubtedly, at least a few of them felt like the fellow in the anecdote about a couple celebrating 50 years together.

The many friends and neighbors who had gathered in for the event had finally left when the wife noticed her husband sitting in his chair, looking morose with his chin against his chest.

"Honey, what's wrong?"

"Oh, I don't know. I just feel so sad."

"But dear," she persisted. "We've had such a lovely time. All those wonderful people. And the gifts. Tell me, what's bothering you?"

"Well, if you must know," he sighed. "Remember some 50 years ago when we were dating and your father walked in on us out in the barn?"

"Oh, yes," she shuddered. "I still can't look Dad in the eye to this very day."

"Well, after you went to the house, your father took me out behind the barn and told me if I didn't marry you, I'd go to prison for 50 years."

"He didn't! Oh, how awful!" the wife wailed, but then gathered her composure.

"But dear, that was 50 years ago. Why are you worrying about that now?"

"I was just thinking," her husband sighed. "I'd be a free man today!"

Seriously, though, unless more of today's couples take Mr. McGeachy's advice and respect each other's "uniqueness," those Sunday photos of people who have been together 50 years will go the way of the dinosaur.

April 1991

You don't have to lay an egg

When I answered my phone, the out-of-town caller asked, "Are you a critic?"

"Oh, yes," I replied. "What do you want criticized?"

Aren't we all critics, even though only a few enjoy the title, the power and the pay? The caller wanted to know if I were the newspaper's book critic, which I am not.

In my salad days, I occasionally reviewed books, even the civic music concert series in Burlington, and, later, some plays at the Raleigh Little Theater.

In most cases, I was kinder than I should have been out of respect for my own ignorance at what I was doing.

Irish playwright Brendan Behan spoke for a lot of wounded actors, authors and, yes, even chefs, when he said, "Critics are like eunuchs in a harem. They're there every night, they see it done every night, they see how it should be done every night, but they can't do it themselves."

I recently attended the Friends of the College ballet at Reynolds Coliseum. From my perch a quarter mile from the stage, I focused my bird-watching binoculars on the dancer.

He was very athletic, leaping hither and yon, lifting the ballerinas as gracefully as a farmer loading 100-pound bags of fertilizer on a pickup truck.

At the end of the number, the crowd of 9,000 or so went wild. "Bravo! Bravo!"

I cased the crowd — a potpourri of people, including babes in arms and toddlers, from Tar Heel farm, village and city.

I couldn't help wondering, "Am I the only lowbrow here who is not moved to foot-stomping 'Bravos!' by what I have just seen?" Sure, ballet is a step up from mud-wrestling. But really.

It's good that I can enjoy art without understanding what makes it great.

Take Van Gogh's "Irises." Nice, though a bit blurred. And I like irises. But worth $50 million, the price supposedly paid by the Getty Museum?

Van Gogh would have been astounded — and furious. The poor preacher-turned-artist ground out 200 paintings in two years, but sold only one before putting a bullet through his head at age 37.

It's not that I don't respect and covet critics' power and skill.

Marilyn Spencer, who for 12 years reviewed restaurants for The News & Observer before recently moving to Charleston, S.C., was a name feared and revered by chefs and restaurant owners.

No Broadway producer or cast awaited a review with greater anticipation and dread than local restaurateurs awaited Marilyn's commentary on their food.

I sometimes disagreed with her. But I respected her opinion. She always cited chapter and verse — overdone fillet, cold croissants, careless waiters — or, on the other hand, superb service and excellent food prepared with flair and intelligence.

Once during an off-duty dinner, Marilyn was asked by a haughty waiter how she and her party enjoyed their meal.

When she told him, he snorted, "Just who do you think you are? Marilyn Spencer?"

"Along with a miserable tip, I left my business card," Marilyn told me.

When I think of critics, I recall an incident attributed to the late opera star, Lauritz Melchior, whose son sat next to me in Latin class at Carolina.

Mr. Melchior was appearing with a Brunnhilde whose voice was not quite up to the strenuous role. In one scene, she appeared on stage on a horse.

Customarily, stage horses are not fed before a performance, and for good reason. But on this occasion, the stable boy had goofed.

The horse committed a terrible faux pas — splat! splat! splat! — right on stage.

As the audience gasped in astonishment, Mr. Melchior rose to the occasion. Turning to the conductor, he shrugged and said, "Everyone is a critic!"

And so we are. After all, you can have an opinion of an omelet without having first to lay an egg.

November 1990

Saying 'I'm sorry' isn't easy

A small, loose association of Surry and Stokes county natives living in Raleigh gets together for lunch once a month to remind ourselves of how lucky we are to have grown up in the foothills.

Normally, much of the meeting is devoted to the unresolved debate over which county had the most humble beginnings and which one God loves the most. In my mind, there is no doubt.

But on our most recent get-together, much of the conversation had to do with a state senator's apology to the Senate and his constituents for his ill-conceived efforts to get a cop fired for ticketing him for not wearing his seat belt.

Some didn't think the apology fit the crime. It came too easy.

The senator, a pretty good public servant over the years, surely must realize by now that the sin of arrogance is one of the most unforgivable.

And he needs to realize that despite all his years of effective service it is, as Shakespeare said: the good men do is "interred with their bones."

The man-on-the-street is in a bad mood these days. Although Senate President Pro Tem Henson Barnes says the Senate doesn't want a pound of flesh from the senator, some of his constituents want him to at least bleed a little.

Both sides of the issue have been well-aired. It is not as Samuel Butler said in defense of the Devil: "It must be remembered that we have only heard one side of the case. God has written all the books."

One mother in our group pointed out that apologizing doesn't come easily to many of us, in fact, not to most of us.

"Take my daughter," she said. "My daughter just got kicked out of Bible camp! I said to her, 'Good Lord, honey, how could you get kicked out of a camp that is operated by people whose whole business is forgiveness? What did you do?'"

"I refused to apologize," the 14-year-old replied.

The mother's younger sister, Jean, overhearing the comment, said, "Just listen to my sister! She's the only person I know who had to stand in the corner for two days when she was 12 years old because she refused to say she was sorry to my dad."

"That wasn't it at all," her sister, Donna, replied. "I asked him if he wanted me to say I was sorry when I wasn't really sorry. But Dad said, no, he wanted me to be truly sorry. And I wasn't."

Don Blackburn, another member of our group, recalled the time when at age 10 he ran into a similar confrontation because he wouldn't say "please."

"My older brothers had gone off to the war and there I was the only son at home on the farm, doing a man's work. I had spent the whole hot morning plowing corn. When I went in to eat lunch, I asked Mom to 'Hand me a biscuit.'

"Dad said, 'Say please, son.'

"And I snapped, 'Look, Dad, I may be 10 years old, but I'm doing a man's work and I don't have to say please to anybody!'

"He then asked me to accompany him to the next room, where he took off his belt and gave me a hiding I remember to this very day. Now, I'll say please anytime you want to hear it and I'll apologize all over the place — even when there's nothing to apologize for."

Not everybody feels that way.

Back in the foothills, a woman I know was emotionally devastated when her husband strayed from the marriage bed for a younger woman. Eventually, he apologized and she outwardly forgave him.

But her heart never totally accepted his apology.

"He never would humble himself," she kept saying bitterly.

Consider George Bush's problem with Saddam Hussein. Saddam never once said he's sorry, despite his humiliating defeat.

And he'll be a thorn in the free world's flesh until he's carried out feet first.

As all of you know, the hardest part of apologizing is the humbling ourselves part, because it eats away at our stubborn pride. And our pride is what constitutes the greater part of our positive self-image.

Pride indeed goeth before a fall, but deprived of pride, only the shell of us remains.

The senator may decide that the job isn't worth "humbling" himself. I can understand that.

August 1992

Showdown with 'Cool Hand'

The very day that Brien Taylor's mother won the $1.55 million showdown with the New York Yankees over the use of her 19-year-old son's strong left arm I was in the final stages of negotiating for a new car.

In effect, Mom Taylor had said to the Yankees, "Look, if you don't come across, I'm going to send my boy to college!"

The Yankees folded.

Mrs. Taylor's "Cool Hand Luke" performance inspired me to get in the car right then and drive out to the Al Smith Buick dealership.

"Take it or leave it," I would say to the stubborn salesman. "I'll just continue to send my wife out into Crabtree Valley traffic in a 1983 Oldsmobile with 68,000 miles!"

It's true that the Taylors were talking about a difference of almost $1 million in what was being offered and what they finally got, while the sticking point between me and the car dealership was more like $275. But the principle and the technique were the same.

Now the New York Yankees' front office is no pussycat. But neither is "Cool Hand Charlie" Capps at Al Smith Buick.

"Aren't you even going to let me make just a little?" he fretted at one point during the standoff.

"Not if I can help it," I replied icily.

My friend Glenn Keever has coached me on how to be a tough-nosed trader.

"You can always tell 'em to forget the under-coating stuff. That's where the hidden fat is."

"Look, I don't need the under-coating stuff," I said, remembering my lines.

"But it comes with the package. You really don't pay anything for it,'" Charlie insisted.

There has always been a certain mystique about car salesmen. The late Harry Golden, in his book, "You're Entitled," describes his own car trading experience.

"You walk back into the office with the salesman who adds the cost of white-wall tires, radio and sun visors, and then takes a deep breath, lifts up that blotter and says, 'We can give you $80 on the old car.'

"He watches your face. If your expression doesn't change, he lifts the blotter up higher, looks around to see that no one is listening, and whispers, 'Make it $120.'

"If you say something to the effect that the dealer on the other side of town offered more, he peeps once again under the blotter, this time with a flashlight, expels his breath like a high diver and says, '$130!'

"If you peek under the blotter while his back is turned, all you'll find is a picture of his wife and kids and a 2-year-old shopping list."

"Cool Hand Charlie" was not like that. He brought on the bear in a hurry. And stuck to his price like tar. I surrendered.

Wandering around the showroom while he filled out the papers, I spotted a "Sales Leader of the Month" wall plaque.

Only one name was on the plaque — seven times, with August still undecided.

"Hey, I'd like to meet Robert," I said to a passing receptionist.

"Oh, he's taking a few days off," she said.

"With that record, he can well afford to. Boy, he must have some kind of charisma!"

"Not necessarily. He just doesn't pressure anybody."

"Well, neither does 'Cool Hand Charlie,'" I said defensively.

When he returned from Hawaii, I called up Robert, the super-salesman.

"Nah, it's not charisma," he insisted modestly.

"I don't pressure people. When someone shows interest in a car, I don't nail their feet to the floor every time they walk in."

That's about all he'd say. I don't blame him for not giving away his secret.

He's probably afraid I might end up as Salesman of the Month for September.

The next time I trade cars I'm going to ask Brien Taylor's Mom to go with me. "Cool Hand Charlie" won't have a chance. Even though he has just been named "Sales Leader of the Month" for August.

September 1991

Back to the cliffs of Dover

It was all we could have hoped for — this first-ever high school reunion of the "only class to graduate in the courthouse because somebody burned the schoolhouse down."

Some of the women cried. A few guys were misty-eyed. My spouse said she enjoyed it more than any of her own three class reunions. It might have been because some guy asked her if she were my second wife.

We met at the Elks Lodge not far from the Mayberry Mall. We played Tommy Dorsey music as 27 of the original 48 graduates relived that long ago May night, when, a few months after Pearl Harbor, we had sung in parting, "There'll be bluebirds over, the white cliffs of Dover, tomorrow, just you wait and see."

I had taken a photostat of The News & Observer front page on the day of our graduation.

The headlines were not hopeful for the 18-year-old male graduates: "Japanese Now Attempting to Land on Corregidor." "Midway Island Repels Attack."

Jennie Martin, our speech and drama teacher, showed up. An innovative 20-year-old graduate of Appalachian State Teacher's College, she had cut her teaching teeth on us — her very first class.

"You were my favorites. I learned with you," she recalled. In my mind I still heard the chanting echo of the Kipling piece she drilled into us:

Boots! Boots! Boots! Boots!
Movin' up and down again
....
Men go mad with watching them!

The reunion program included a list of the senior superlatives.

Foy Parker, voted "most romantic boy," had married Betty Folger, "most romantic girl."

"You must have been right when you voted me the most romantic and most athletic," Foy said. "Betty and I have six kids."

I was listed as "most studious" and "most likely to succeed." I never considered myself in either category.

I had much rather have been voted "most romantic." But "making out" isn't easy when you are afflicted with a world-class case of acne. During the reunion, I kept glancing at the two girls I had loved from afar in the 11th grade.

Should I tell them, after all these years, that they were the wind beneath my wings in senior high? I decided not to.

"I always remembered you standing against the radiator reading a book," an unremembered classmate said.

"That must have been in first grade," I corrected her. The only time I remember standing against the radiator was during that winter of my discontent when the teacher refused to excuse me to go to the toilet.

It is an inexperienced teacher who gambles when little boys say they have to "go." I went. At my seat.

During recess, when I sidled over to the radiator to dry off, a pungent odor permeated the room. The angry teacher threw open all the windows, which only served to let in freezing air and to intensify my embarrassment.

John Witt, the class mischief-maker, asked me to autograph a program for his 11-year-old son Dudley, who has seen my mug in The News & Observer over in Ahoskie.

I gladly complied, identifying with the lad, since I, too, was a love child, growing up with an older father. But John still seemed to have all the energy and wit and zest that my father had long spent when I came along.

I did not count the Cadillacs in the parking lot to see who was "most successful." I did not note a single mink coat.

Nevertheless, I left the Elks Lodge with the feeling that we all felt we had well weathered life's storms. Not one walked with a cane. All seemed self-assured, all mentally alert, all well dressed.

Perhaps it was only the magic of our first time together after half a century. But on this one November night, the bluebirds had come back to the white cliffs of Dover and we were 18 again.

November 1992

Fathers in a field of dreams

My friend Mel Finch told me recently that he is going to fly off to Las Vegas for a weekend with his married son. Just the two of them. I reminded him that his son is paying him the highest of compliments.

"Oh, yes, I'm much closer to him now at 36 than I ever was when we were growing up," he said.

Another Raleigh friend, Fred Crisp Jr., recalls the death of his mother and his father's reaction to the loss of his mate.

"We were always so close to Mom that I am sure that, when she died, Dad thought we would abandon him altogether," Fred said.

"I remember when we were picking out Mother's marker. I didn't much like what he liked. But when I suggested something else, he lost his temper and said, 'Son, dammit! Can't I even pick out my wife's tombstone?'"

"I later learned why he was insistent on the one we ended up getting. It had space for his name on it, along with the usual date of birth, etc. He knew that he would end up beside her, where he had always been."

This is that time of year when fathers and sons should be asking in their hearts, as Browning asked Browning, "How do I love thee? Let me count the ways."

It is high time for such an inventory. A recent Gallup Poll asked 3,000 people to name their best friend. Not one mentioned Dad. Not one! Obviously, dads aren't doing so well.

I particularly enjoy the TV commercial in which a young father drives his small son out into the country. They park beside an open field and watch a jet as it takes off from a nearby airport and flies off into the sunset.

The little boy runs across the field, waving his arms up and down like the wings of the plane. The father watches, adoration in his eyes.

It is not only a good commercial for the airlines. It is a good message of togetherness for men who are or will become fathers.

In a Raleigh apartment building that is home to a lot of senior citizens, a wiry old fellow and a younger man share the elevator with me.

As they step off the elevator at the ground floor, the young man, preparing to leave, pats the older man on the shoulder and says reassuringly, "Dad, you're going to be fine, just fine."

There was so much affection in the simple statement that I wished I could capture the sound and send it to all the lonely old men who, their mates gone before them, are making it alone in the world on this Father's Day.

In the movie, "Field of Dreams," Kevin Costner's father comes back to life and is standing by the corn rows that border the baseball field in Iowa.

Costner sees his father as he was in his youth "before I was even a glint in his eye, before life wore him down."

I envied him that moment. My father was 64 when I was born, too worn down to take me fishing, to tired teach me how to catch a baseball or to give the self-assurance small boys cry out for.

It wasn't his fault. And it wasn't all bad. Instead of chasing fly balls in my field of dreams, I become a chaser of words and thoughts. But I wonder what my father was like as a young man. My mother, 20 years younger, says he was handsome and "well off," and one of the best catches in the county.

But you have to take with a grain of salt what a woman in love tells you. Even though I was 14 when he died, my father was a man I never really knew.

Marcus Mabry, a Newsweek Magazine staffer, in a recent article on vanishing fathers, wrote about growing up without the father who abandoned his mother during pregnancy, married someone else and became a prominent judge and community leader.

Now trying to establish a relationship with his father, Mabry writes, "He called two weeks in a row this month. I felt lucky, even grateful.

"Really. I know I have every reason to be angry and bitter for what he has not given me. But even now, and maybe forever, what I really want is a father."

So say we all, every one of us.

June 1992

Finally, the fat lady sang

I can't seem to get that song out of my head. I heard it when I flipped on the radio on the way home from work and heard Tammy Faye's frantic voice rising in song a few moments after the jury delivered its "guilty on all counts" verdict.

On Christ the solid rock I stand
All other ground is sinking sand.

Was this haunting rendition of a song my mother used to sing the performance of an accomplished actress? Or was it the soul of someone in the wilderness, crying out in torment?

For a moment I was almost caught up in the spell that has booby-trapped the minds of so many good people across our land, and has milked millions from Social Security checks as well as from hefty bank accounts.

On the day before the Jim Bakker verdict, a reader called to express regret over the approaching demise of The Raleigh Times, of which I have been a part for 31 years, including 16 as editor.

She also admitted to being a loyal reader of this column.

"I never called you before," she said. "I just wanted you to know I love you."

I thanked her. We don't get many calls like that. Especially from strangers.

"And I love that old News and Observer, too." she added. We get even fewer calls like that. But she sounded cold sober.

"And I love Jim and Tammy Bakker — with all my heart," she added. That gave me cause for pause. Her love suddenly seemed too all-inclusive.

My caller was not your typical Jim and Tammy disciple.

"I lived next door to the Bakkers in Portsmouth, Va., for 14 years," she said. "No two finer people have walked the face of the earth. They were such a nice young couple. And they lived plain and gave what they had to the Lord."

"But what about all that money, all that greed, all that deception?"

"All lies. Gold doorknobs? Ha! I got gold doorknobs. They look like gold doorknobs. But they're just brass. I doubt Jim and Tammy's doorknobs were solid gold. Maybe just gold-plated.

"Anyway, you folks have been a lot nicer to Jim and Tammy than another newspaper I could mention," she said, referring to The Charlotte Observer.

"But God punished that city. He sent Hurricane Hugo to Charlotte. 'Vengeance is mine, saith the Lord.' "

I passed the last bit of information on to a friend who said, "She's right about God pushing Hugo to Charlotte. But he was aiming at Jim Bakker. Poor Charlotte just got in the way."

I am surprised and troubled by the reaction to the Bakker fiasco by some members of the legitimate clergy.

For example, the Rev. Bill Finlator was quoted as saying, "All ministers share in Mr. Bakker's guilt because if they had been giving the real Gospel message, folks wouldn't have been taken in by a phony TV message."

Horsefeathers, Reverend! Eight years ago, we had a Bakker-type scandal in our profession.

A Washington Post reporter by the name of Janet Cooke won a Pulitzer Prize for a heart-wrenching story about an 8-year-old boy who was being injected with heroin by his mother's boyfriend.

The reporter described how she actually saw the needle being shoved into the kid's arm.

Ms. Cooke wouldn't tell her editors her sources, identify the kid or the boyfriend. Her editors went right along with her, even to her refusing to share information with police so they could rescue the youngster.

Well, as you remember, Ms. Cooke eventually confessed that she had made up the whole thing, and the Post had to give back its Pulitzer.

A lot of editors and columnists went around moaning that the entire journalism profession had been tainted by this one incident. Not I.

I agree with what columnist Mike Royko said at the time:

"Nuts!" he snorted. "Only the Washington Post is tainted by this shabby affair.

"After all, when Bradlee, Woodward, Bernstein and the Post became national idols because of Watergate, they didn't say that the rest of us were also national idols. Now that they're bums, they can keep the distinction for themselves too."

Mr. Finlator and the good preachers that we all know — from those in the big downtown sanctuaries to the ones in the little crossroads churches beside the cornfields of rural America — haven't received one dime of the millions the Bakkers have collected.

So they're under no obligation whatsoever to share in the landslide of guilt and punishment.

Tammy Faye insists that "It ain't over until it's over." Maybe she's right.

But I like better the version by Dick Motta, former coach of the Washington Bullets: "It ain't over until the Fat Lady sings."

Well, that day driving home, I'm pretty sure I heard the Fat Lady singing on WPTF-AM.

October 1989

Bad dogs in Paradise

Across the mist of years, I hear faintly a fiddler's hoedown square-dancing tune that goes something like this:
Granny, will your dog bite?
No, child, no.
Granny, will your dog bite?
Do si doe.

So what does Granny know? Nothing. Up in Surry County there is a dog that doesn't like me, a dog that came out of nowhere and took a Big Mac bite out of my left leg as I was walking along a rural road with my sister and her friend, Izella Fleming.

Now, I know how postmen feel. Now I, who have loved dogs all my life, who never carried a stick to ward off one, know a new fear. And it is not pleasant.

Neither was the pain, nor the sight of blood gushing from the punctured leg, nor the long wait at Elkin Hospital's emergency room to which Izella had rushed me, speeding along the winding roads, dashing through the dusk illuminated by the white ghosts of flowering dogwood.

In the waiting room where misfortune, great and small, has brought us together, I try to stanch the bleeding with a paper towel.

"He was bitten by a dog," my sister says, in answer to the inquiring stares of the assembled strangers.

"Did the dog die?" wisecracks a stout woman across the room.

When no one laughs, she adds apologetically, "I didn't mean no harm."

I remember a few years ago when my neighbor Ed Green, vacationing in Florida, was riding his bike across a bridge when he was bitten by a dog.

He received treatment from a local doctor, and the sheriff ordered the owner to keep the dog penned for three weeks.

I was at Ed's house when the letter from the owner came. It said simply, "Our dog did not get sick. I hope you are doing all right."

Every emergency room is alike. My treatment was delayed by real emergencies, a man having a heart attack, a woman being rushed back into the ambulance for a trip to Winston-Salem, an elderly woman who, according to her daughter, has a problem in which her blood pressure fluctuates from 180 to 0 — if that's possible.

In my case, the young doctor, deciding not to take stitches, ordered a tetanus shot. He then filled out a form that he said would be turned over to the county's animal control department.

"What was the dog's name?"

"I don't know," I said. "We were never formally introduced."

I later learned the dog — a bulldog — is called Brownie.

The contrite owners insisted Brownie has never before even offered to bite anyone.

Then why me?

"It was probably because you were from Raleigh," one fellow observed dryly. "Up here, dogs will eat anything from Raleigh — especially when the legislature is in session."

I don't know why I was bitten. Only Brownie knows for sure and he's not talking until he sees his lawyer. I like to think that Brownie was just having a bad day and smelled a stranger.

As the two women with me agreed, "It could have been worse."

"He could have bitten one of us," one said later. "At least A.C.'s pants leg will cover his scar."

I called my wife in Raleigh to report the incident.

"I didn't know there were any bad dogs in Paradise," she chuckled, after sympathizing with my plight.

"Even St. Peter isn't perfect," I said. "A few bad eggs get through now and then."

The owner said he would destroy Brownie. I interceded halfheartedly in the dog's behalf, but that was before I learned his wife keeps small children. Now I don't know. Anyway, the decision is not mine.

But in the future, I will beware of all dogs, even Granny's. And I am sorry for that.

April 1991

Trouble with a capital 'T'

I encountered the little girl and her dad at the Fairgrounds Flea Market, where I had gone with my older daughter, Melinda, and her friend Larrissa, who were home for the holiday.

The child, no more than 4, stood transfixed before a cage of restless rabbits and crawling kittens, murmuring over and over "I need that kitty."

"Not today, honey," said the father, in his late 20s, tugging at her hand.

Five minutes later, they were back, the child pointing to the same white kitten with gray-tipped ears and tail, and saying, "Daddy, I need that kitty."

"Not right now, honey," the father pleaded.

"You're a goner," I said. "A moment ago, it was 'not today.'"

He ran up the white flag on the third visit, asking the woman to keep the kitten while he went to his car for a checkbook.

But an hour later the kitten was still in its cage.

"He said he had to check with his wife's mother," the woman explained. "The little girl lives with her grandmother."

Ah, yes, Murphy Brown. Single parenthood isn't simple. Even for the non-poor, merely adopting a kitten.

It was not a question of affording, but a matter of inconveniencing not one of the parents, but the grandmother, an innocent bystander.

Dan Quayle has done us a favor by sparking this debate. How can we assume that everyone who sits down to watch Murphy Brown or, yes, even the Cosby Show, knows that it's only make-believe?

When 38 million people are glued to a single episode of "let's pretend" and great numbers — including impressionable teenagers — accept it as real life, we have trouble in River City.

TV is a powerful common denominator, becoming more common every day.

My daughter, who works in animal research at a major hospital, daily monitors a large room filled with monkeys. Yes, even the monkeys watch TV.

"They are hooked on two particular programs — the 'Donahue' show in the morning and 'Teen Age Mutant Ninja Turtle' in the afternoon. If I switch channels during one of these, they become very hostile, hooting at me and rattling their cages."

This, she explained, has more to do with animation than the ratings. On "Donahue" you have all those women yelling back and forth and the Turtle cartoons, of course, are very colorful and animated.

"Have you offered them 'Murphy Brown?'" I suggested. How can 35 million humans and a room full of apes be wrong?

"No, it comes on too late," she said.

The decision to opt for single parenting, or to come by it through accident or lack of choice, rarely is one of those "It's my life" decisions. The burden of responsibility — emotional and financial — of a child overflows all over other people.

While at the flea market, my single adult daughter, against my advice, bought a tiny Siamese kitten. She already has a French poodle.

Sure, it's her decision, her life. But when she goes on vacation or even comes home for a visit, others are affected. She does not like to leave her "children" in the kennel.

Think how much more complex it is when the kitten is a child, which can't be checked into the kennel for a weekend or left at the SPCA. Somewhere in Wake County today, a grandmother has a kitten to care for, in addition to a child.

On Monday morning before leaving, my daughter came up to my bedroom for one of our father-daughter chats. The kitten, she said, had kept her awake most of the night with its mewing and moving about.

"I felt like bashing her," she laughed.

I swallowed my "I told you so."

"What have you named it?" I asked.

"Trouble," she said, her eyes twinkling. "I named her 'Trouble.'"

"You could have named her 'Murphy Brown,'" I said.

May 1992

A 'bodice ripper' to remember

I stumbled across "The Bridges of Madison County" by Robert James Waller well before it became fashionable to drop the title at bridge clubs and cocktail parties.

"Oh, have you read 'Bridges of Madison County?'" it goes, and the answer is either "No, I haven't, but it's at the top of my list" or "Yes, I have, and wouldn't you just love to visit the farm in Iowa?"

Despite Doonesbury's low opinion of it, the little volume is a winner. It's the kind of heart-tugging story you like to store in a corner of your brain to recall on a bad day turned as sour as a pickle.

The Wake County library system has purchased 279 copies of the book and still can't satisfy the demand. Three million hardcover copies of the 171-page volume will be in print at year's end.

Remember a few years ago when "Lucille," a haunting, unhappy country song just as popular as this book, touched on this same theme of loneliness that leads to infidelity.

You picked a fine time to leave me, Lucille,
With four hungry children and a crop in the field.

You have to have lived on a farm to fully appreciate the plight of a hardworking farmer, abandoned by a wife who no longer can bear the boredom, the hard work and the specter of an unchanging path to the grave.

What kind of a woman leaves a guy with four kids to feed and bathe, nobody to cuddle up to at night or help harvest the crop by day?

She could have at least waited until the tobacco was in the barn.

Lucille does not come off nearly as well as the wife in "The Bridges of Madison County."

Except for that three-day fling while her husband was away from the farm, this wife remained loyal to her spouse ever after.

In U.S. News and World Report, John Leo describes the book as a "bodice ripper that has gone mainstream."

If that's what it is, it's several cuts above the rash of bodice rippers being ground out these days. "Bodice rippers" are big business. I read somewhere that in 1991, the average romance novel addict spent $1,200 on such books.

In "Bridges," Robert Kincaid is a free-lance photographer who goes to Iowa to photograph several rural bridges. He happens to stop by a farmhouse for directions and bingo!, he's smitten by the woman who answers his knock.

I've known a lot of photographers in my time, but none who seemed to measure up to Robert Kincaid on the sensitivity scale. The guy is really sensitive.

As Leo says, "We know he's sensitive because he cleans the tub himself after taking a bath, and he closes the screen door quietly instead of letting it slam like all Iowa males do."

This book's appeal must be due in part to the Iowa farm setting, although the stereotype of Iowa farm wives prohibits their going around having affairs with itinerant shutterbugs.

The farm wife I knew best — my mother — would never have considered an extramarital affair. Even if she were inclined, when would she have found the opportunity? With whom would she have it?

The preacher? Never. Even if she had been tempted, she knew that lusting after a man of the cloth would bring down God's wrath on her quicker than she could catch a chicken, wring its neck and dress it for the parson's Sunday dinner.

The only other man in her life, outside her family, was the Watkins product salesman who came by the farm periodically to peddle liniment, vanilla flavoring and the like.

Whatever affection she might have harbored for the "Watkins man" vanished the day the poor fellow backed his A-model Ford over the well-house. My brothers had to be fetched from the field to hitch up the horses and pull the car off the well. The salesman never came back.

Free-lance writer, Pauli Carnes, in the Los Angles Times, calls "The Bridges of Madison County" "pornography for middle-aged women."

"Ladies," she says, "a little reality check here: No one is going to drive up to your door and rescue your life from dreariness. You made the ruts of your life — take a little responsibility for yourself!"

Hold on there, Pauli. Times are a'changing. Today's farm wives aren't what they used to be.

They now have the spirit, the means and the transportation to hop a plane to New York or Raleigh, go shopping at Tiffany's or Hudson Belk's, enjoy a couple of Broadway plays or a Friends of the College concert and come home with a head stuffed full of all kinds of crazy ideas.

So if you're a farmer out on the South Forty, disking under those dead tobacco stalks and you see a pickup truck pull into the driveway up at the house, get up there right away.

It may be some "sensitive" photographer asking directions to that old bridge over on the Neuse River.

October 1993

Donaldson didn't do Fairmont

As the youngest in a large family, I was always regarded as the "dreamer." I wasn't much help in the fields and was a total washout at anything mechanical. My older brothers didn't see how I could ever amount to much.

But they tolerated me with patience, partly because, like the brothers of Jacob's son, Joseph, they dared not lay a hand on me.

I had no coat of many colors, but I was the apple of my mother's eye, even in her big orchard of children.

At times, they undoubtedly would have cheerfully sold me to some passing merchant if they had thought they could have gotten away with it.

They were right about my being a dreamer. But in a different context. Every night, I grind out one meaningless Grade-B mini-drama after another.

Although a friend insists that no dream is without meaning, I don't agree.

Here are reruns of three dreams I remembered after a recent night's restless sleep.

In the first, TV news anchorman Sam Donaldson blew into town on his way to Fairmont where Sam Donaldson Day was being observed.

Donaldson dropped by the newspaper, looked me up and asked me to help write a poem he wanted to read for the occasion.

In the next dream, I was shampooing my hair — what's left of it — at work. When I reached for my hairbrush, it was missing.

Walking down the hall, I met one of our young reporters, who said, "Oh, incidentally, A.C., your hairbrush is in my car." No explanation whatsoever.

Then I dreamed I was playing Mozart at Carnegie Hall — to a standing ovation. The only piano I ever went near was the player-piano I grew up with in Surry County.

None of this makes sense. I'm not a Sam Donaldson man — I'm a Dan Rather person. Besides, Donaldson hails from El Paso, Texas, not Fairmont, N.C.

Never in my 34 years at The News & Observer have I even showered, much less washed my hair, at work. And I have never left my hairbrush in anybody's car, least of all a woman's.

Not being a God-inspired interpreter of dreams like Joseph, I mentioned the three plots to a friend, who is seldom at a loss for answers to anything.

"First, the hairbrush," he said. "Subconsciously, you wish you had left your hairbrush in some woman's car. Clearly, this is latent, subconscious rebellion over your abiding fidelity to your wife. Beware.

"As for the Carnegie Hall concert, you have admitted your lifelong frustration over never having scored a touchdown in Kenan Stadium — or anywhere else, for that matter.

"You have transferred this suppressed desire to a piano concert — which is more your speed, although you would be more at home in Reynolds Coliseum plunking a banjo and singing "Blue Tail Fly" than doing Mozart at Carnegie Hall."

Even he couldn't interpret the Sam Donaldson dream. But I finally did.

I remembered that a few days earlier, while cleaning out some old files, I came across a letter from Dan Rather dated Jan. 3, 1977.

In it, he thanked me for a column item I had written just after the 1976 presidential election. I had commented on the neat way that Rather, then a rising star on the CBS horizon, signed off after it was clear Jimmy Carter had defeated Gerald Ford.

He had said something like, "Well, boys, it's all over. You can call off the dogs and pour water on the fire." The original version, though, was considerably more earthy.

It's my opinion that most dreams have their origin in incidents that occur during our waking moments. The problem is that while the brain sleeps, the plots bounce about in the subconscious like ping-pong balls.

If Joseph's future fate had depended on his making sense of my dreams, he would have died in Pharaoh's prison.

February 1992

Why not just say 'fish?'

During the short and satisfactory Persian Gulf war, I heard Vice President Dan Quayle say that Saddam Hussein should take a cue from King Belshazzar, the famous fellow who read the very first "handwriting on the wall."

Mr. Quayle's Biblical allusion undoubtedly fell on fallow ground with most listeners under 30, who likely would identify Belshazzar as a new hard rock group. The only handwriting on the wall many know is the graffiti on toilet walls of service stations between here and the beach.

I doubt that even Mr. Quayle recalls the mysterious message: "Mene , Mene, tekel, upharsin," which Daniel interpreted in part as "God has numbered the days of your kingdom and brought it to an end..."

Because of the generation gap and the general mishmash of gobbledygook and bureaucratic jargon in our language, we communicate within a veritable Tower of Babel.

But it's not a new problem.

My older sister, Ima, recently recalled a communication problem with a certain patient during her nurse's training days at a Mount Airy hospital.

An uneducated mountain woman had came to the hospital with a complicated pregnancy. The doctor, trying to establish the date of conception, asked her about her menstrual cycle.

Confused by the term, the woman turned to my sister, who whispered an explanation.

"Oh," the woman said. "The last time I saw anything was at fodder pulling time."

This time, it was Dr. Martin who was confused.

"Miss Ima," he said. "Could you translate that for me?"

"Early September," my sister answered. In September the farmers performed the onerous task of stripping the dying blades from the corn stalks, binding and storing them for winter feeding of livestock.

Dr. Bill Simpson, pastor at Edenton Street Methodist Church, has a minister friend who is a CB addict. His handle is "Ichthys."

"This is Ichthys, signing off," he said one day. A trucker somewhere out there in CB-land drawled, "Say that again, good buddy?"

"Ichthys. It's the Greek word for fish," the minister explained.

"Well, good buddy," said the trucker, "why don't you just say fish?"

Yes, why don't we say what we mean? Why don't we care as much as Noah Webster did about word choices?

Mr. Webster, the story goes, was fooling around with his secretary when his wife walked in.

Aghast at the sight of the secretary sitting on her husband's lap, Mrs. Webster gasped, "Noah, I am surprised at you."

"No, my dear," said the careful word merchant, "You are astonished. We are surprised."

Of course we shouldn't be so prissily correct that we destroy the rich flavor of colloquial expression.

I once read in a column by Jack Smith of the Los Angeles Times in which a reader defended baseball manager Sparky Anderson's characteristic abuse of grammar.

"Only a cretin," he said "would destroy the music of one of Sparky Anderson's multiple negatives in "It don't take no genius, Vinnie, to figure that no pitcher's gonna throw no lollipop to no Mike Marshall when he's on a hot streak."

Then there's the other extreme — outlandish verbosity — such as you find in this little exercise:

"A warm-blooded vertebrate of the class avis grasped in the terminal prehensile portion of the upper limb of the human body is equal in value to one plus one of the aforementioned vertebrates in a shrub."

That's how a doctoral thesis at one of our universities might say "A bird in the hand is worth two in the bush."

The trucker was right. Why don't we just say "fish?"

March 1991

Dads don't always know best

An Iowa woman recently wrote Ann Landers about fathers who interfere when they don't approve of the men their daughters choose to love.

Her father intensely disliked her high school boyfriend, who always went around with a toothpick between his teeth. He never called him by name, but always groused, "Are you going out with Toothpick tonight?"

I sent the clipping to my older daughter, who once dated a young man I liked a lot. He was relaxed, easygoing and owned a pickup truck. A young man with a pickup truck is prime son-in-law material for the father of two mobile, college-age daughters.

"I'm sorry, Daddy," she said, when I complained about the break-up. "I know you like his rural background, his easygoing personality and all that. But I just couldn't stand the toothpicks."

The Iowa woman said her father's dislike of her boyfriend only made her more determined to keep him. She was a college freshman when the fellow pressured her to run off with him to get married. He proposed with a toothpick in his mouth.

"Suddenly it hit me that I would probably have to look at a piece of wood stuck between his teeth for the rest of my life," she wrote.

She rejected the offer. He became angry and kicked the cat on the way out the door.

One day, three years later, her dad called.

"Well, Toothpick's picture is in the paper," he said. "He robbed a bank."

The woman concluded her letter with "I guess Daddies always know best."

On June 7, amid the media hoopla marking the 50th anniversary of D-Day, a reader called to ask if I could provide the name of the newspaper in a California city. She wanted to return a pair of silver paratrooper wings to a Californian she had met, loved, married and lost during World War II.

She lost her man not to battle, but to meddling parents. She was 17 when, on a church picnic at Raleigh's Pullen Park, she met the handsome young Fort Bragg soldier. In the face of her parents' opposition, they eventually eloped to South Carolina.

"I was just a little country girl and they couldn't see their baby moving to California," she said with bitterness in her voice. So afterwards, they saw each other only rarely, when her parents were not around or when she could meet him somewhere briefly for a few hours. His letters to her were intercepted. She was forced to divorce him.

She last saw her young husband in November 1943, only months before he participated in the Normandy invasion.

Now, with her second husband and parents deceased, she felt this great urgency to return the man's paratrooper wings.

I gave her the name of the newspaper, but suggested she might have more success by just calling Information and asking for the guy's telephone number.

A few hours later, she called me at home, her voice trembling with emotion.

"I located his brother," she said. "We had a good visit. He told me Danny died last year on Guam, where he lived with the woman he married only four years ago. He had not re-married for all those years. I am sending the wings to his brother."

For half a century she had resisted the longing to contact the man she said she loved above all others. D-Day's anniversary had given her the courage to close this painful chapter in her life.

Yes, she admitted, it had crossed her mind that he might still be single or a widower, and that they might pick up where they left off.

"I never got over what my parents did to me," she said sadly.

A good friend recently recalled that her parents did not welcome with enthusiasm the news of her engagement. They never said a word against the fiance. They just couldn't stop talking about the hometown guy she had stopped dating.

Hearing that their daughter was ill, the sensitive parents worried that they might have been in some way responsible. They suddenly appeared, unannounced, on their daughter's doorstep in Raleigh after a long drive across eastern North Carolina.

"They put their arms around me and told me that if I loved him and he loved me, that was all that mattered. And they meant it," she said. "Then, thirty minutes later, they got into their car and drove the long trip back home."

The marriage was a long and happy one. The husband was adored by her parents.

No, daddies don't always know best. Most do the best they can, raising their children by trial and error, which is fine — up to a point. But when it comes to interfering in the matter of whom their children choose to love, interfering fathers are on dangerous ground.

June 1994

Judged by the way we speak

One of several responses to a recent column on racism came from Dr. Morris Thompson, poet laureate of Rocky Mount. "I read your wonderful piece on racism," he wrote. "Being Irish, tears came to my eyes. A black mother with a fine-looking son sat across from us at Hardee's as I read your piece on Saturday morning.

"We had spoken to each other and exchanged 'Nice days!' I felt compelled to hand her your column. She and her son read it. She thanked me with a warm smile and looked away while reaching for her handkerchief.

"It has often been truly said that we are born without prejudices and are taught them. Much of my grade school life was spent in a middle class neighborhood in Trenton, Missouri, a railroad terminal point.

"I remember my four best friends. Dale was red-headed, so he was 'Red.' Frank was just 'Frank.' I was fat, so I was 'Tubby.' The one black friend was Joseph, so he was 'Nigger Joe.'

"Neither Joe nor any of us knew that nasty six-letter word, as you aptly called it, was anything other than a nickname, just like 'Tubby.' But as we matured, we learned otherwise."

As Dr. Thompson points out, most of us have suffered childhood taunts. In second grade, I was called "Four Eyes" because I wore glasses. After a couple days of torment, on the way home from school, I took care of the problem by tossing the glasses out the bus window.

My folks couldn't afford a second pair. I didn't wear glasses again until 25 years later. Unfortunately, not every kid can terminate his torment so easily.

A troubling response came from a highly articulate woman who spoke with a rich Spanish accent. I sensed her intelligence well before I learned she is a university teacher, speaks four languages and attended prep school in England.

"Before my husband and I moved here, we were told by our friends, 'You aren't going to like North Carolina. Those people speak funny.' I kept hearing things like this over and over until I had a hard time thinking of Southerners as intelligent people.

"How wrong they were. We found the area lovely and the people very nice. And, of course, I now know that a Southern accent doesn't equate to being dumb. It was such an odd idea in the first place. But now I have a similar problem in North Carolina. I am treated differently because I, a Puerto Rican, speak with a Spanish accent."

In search of something to control an allergy, she consulted a pharmacist, who in explaining the drug, started to mention "desensitize."

"But he caught himself, thinking, 'Oh, this is such a big word for her,' and started defining the term.

"In a bookstore, I was looking for a book by Andy Rooney. A salesclerk said 'Now this is only a compilation' and then proceeded to define 'compilation.' This happens to me all the time."

Prejudice has many faces. I am the victim of a soft-spoken voice, which leads some people to believe I lack fire or force. They tend to "tape-over" me in group conversations. All soft-spoken men know of what I speak.

President Lyndon Johnson once asked Press Secretary Bill Moyers to say the blessing at a White House luncheon.

"Speak up Bill! I can't hear a damned thing!" Johnson interrupted.

"I wasn't addressing you, Mr. President," replied the soft-spoken Moyers.

We are even stereotyped by our religious affiliation. Baptists are regarded as the sparrows of the ecclesiastical flock; Episcopalians come across as the elitist nightingales.

The Baptist image has suffered from the open-shop policy that for years allowed almost anyone to take to the pulpit. Too many Baptist preachers have mistakenly thought the "GPC" they envisioned in the sky meant "Go Preach Christ," when, in reality, it merely meant "Go Plow Corn."

We all have our pride of prejudices. I form negative opinions of people who chew gum in church.

Rather than importing Singapore's bloody caning practice, we should adopt its law against selling gum. No one has ever established a good reason for gum, except to make Wrigley rich.

From birth to the grave, we'll confront prejudice, most of which we can survive through a sense of self-worth and perseverance. Unfortunately, some strains are so virulent they impose long-term suffering and set up roadblocks to what we like to call "the good life."

May 1994

'This is something I raised'

I have read the 48 entries in the Ad-Pak's "Why My Dad is No. 1" contest. I have my own list of winners.

One is 8-year-old Daniel Williamson Jr., who wrote: "I think my father is No. 1 because he is best in hardware. He can make tulips and all kinds of things."

Ah, there's the complete man — practical, yet sensitive. One who can change the spark plugs and also grow a tulip.

Not only children, but also women, will beat a path to the door of Frank Olafson of Raleigh, about whom his daughter, Amy, said: "He makes waffles on Sunday. He squirts us with the garden hose, too. He tickles us, too."

Every kid needs a father she can trust, one like 6-year-old Christina Walton's:

"He keeps promises, he tells the truth."

A true test of fathering is how the man conducts himself when the going gets rough.

Twelve-year-old Amber Frazier's father must be a real winner: "My dad is No. 1 because when we went bankrupt, he still found time for my brother, mom and I. He has always been there when I needed him."

Reading the children's entries brought a nostalgic ache, a harking back to another time. It didn't help when I dropped by the mail room and Ron Price regaled me with the details of coaching his 3-year-old Melissa to victory in her preschool's Olympics egg race.

Standing tall when the kids are small is as easy as falling off a log. You have no real competition, except for Mom, and you can work around that.

It's when they reach 12 or 13, that you begin to shrink. And when they're in their late teens, you really have to sweat for even a six or seven on the Richter scale of fatherhood.

Over lunch not long ago, two fathers were complaining about their sons.

"When I went to the freezer, he'd been there before me and had wiped out a whole box of my Oreos," said Ambrose Dudley.

"Isn't it enough that they wear your clothes, drive your car and nearly run you crazy? So now, they also eat your Oreos!"

"Yeah, I know," Dave Jones sympathized. "I finally wised up and started locking my snacks in the trunk of my car. But to be really sure, you should store your Oreos in a lockbox, bury it in the back yard and plant a rhododendron on top of it."

When I was a youngster, I regarded the father of the Prodigal Son in

Why not call me 'Mister?'

A couple of months after I acquired my first and only son-in-law, his wife came to me and said, "Daddy, do you mind if Adam calls you A.C.?"

I was caught off guard. In spite of all the preparation and excitement of the wedding, that was one bridge I had not even thought about crossing.

"Let me think about it," I said, a little lamely.

"Well, I call his parents Carter and Betsy," she said. "And they don't mind."

I can't explain why I had any reservation in granting such a simple request. After all, total strangers, either on the phone or in letters, address me as A.C. and I rarely resent it.

I do, however, react negatively when someone uses familiarity as a foot in the door for a telephone sales speech.

You've experienced the same thing. The phone rings and someone says, "Hi, A.C., how are you doing? How is the weather in Raleigh? Did you have a good Christmas? How are the kids?"

All the while I'm thinking, who is this? Ralph? My long-lost college roommate? Or Tommy, the guy we got to know on the trip to Europe?

Then, after the fellow launches his sales pitch for contributions to the "Society to Save America From Liberalism" or "The International Foundation for Maligned Meter Readers" and I realize he's calling from New York City or Miami, I bid him a firm goodbye and hang up.

Not long ago, Washington Post columnist William Raspberry addressed the matter of first-name familiarity.

He had been annoyed by a flight attendant who went from passenger to passenger in the first-class section asking them how they wished to be addressed.

"All the other men answered with Bob or Jim or Kenneth. She seemed taken aback when I answered, 'Mr. Raspberry,'" the columnist wrote.

Mr. Raspberry (I doubt he would want me to address him as "Bill," although we have met from time to time) included a comment from "Having Our Say," a best seller we both have read.

In it, the Delany sisters, Dr. Elizabeth Delany, 102, and sister Sarah, 104, said they resented being called by their first names "as if we were children or no-account."

I'm not surprised. They grew up in the South and attended St. Augustine's College here in Raleigh, and it's understandable that many blacks would have objected to being addressed by their first names.

However, in my case, being addressed as "Snow" has been particu-

the Bible as the ideal parent.

Think about it. A totally irresponsible young man walks off the farm with the crops still in the field, and blows his inheritance on wine, women and whatever else was going on in those days.

Then he comes dragging home, tail between his legs, broke, dirty, half-naked. And his father rushes out to meet him, throws his arms around the boy and reinstates him fully.

Yes, that really impressed me back then. But today's dads do the very same thing all the time and get no publicity whatsoever.

When the Chicago Bulls won the NBA championship Wednesday night, I thought of Michael Jordan's father. What a Father's Day gift!

And what a comment from Jordan's father. Sitting in the locker room with his arm around his weeping son, he said proudly to reporters, "This is something I raised."

No matter if it's a superstar soaring to impossible heights, or a daughter, head held high, walking across the stage in her cap and gown.

Or a son or daughter who has sacrificed a summer to a hard, back-breaking job.

Or even a prodigal son, coming home from college with four C's and a D and the tail pipe on his jalopy dragging on the driveway.

Like it or not, you can't deny the heart, which skips a beat and whispers to the soul, "This is something I raised."

June 1991

larly irritating to me over the years. I once shared my peeve with a neighbor who addressed me that way.

"I just happen to like the name 'Snow,'" he said, puzzled. But all my life, including my sojourn in the Air Force, I suffered the same sense of put-down over the use of my last name, pretty much as the Delany sisters did about being addressed by their first names.

Perhaps that's why I am probably too prone to call new acquaintances by their first names, including some of you readers who call or write. I figure that if I have written something that has moved you to contact me personally, we already have reached a first-name relationship.

The same day the Raspberry column ran in our newspaper, I caught myself addressing by her first name a Hudson Belk employee who, with infinite patience, has helped me with so many purchases. I no longer call her by her first name.

How to address your minister or doctor or others who occupy a unique position in your life is a problem for many people.

The difficulty may arise from the awe in which we tend to hold those who we think have the ability to save soul or body from the ravages of sin and disease. Yet if we can comfortably address God as God, why not Bill as Bill? Or Frank as Frank?

Southerners are more inclined than others to quickly establish lines of familiarity. But even then, there are exceptions. My aunt called her husband "Mr. Holder" from the day they married. He, in turn, referred to her as "Miss Fannie." Still, the formal address did not prevent the couple from begetting and birthing several children.

As for the in-law business, I asked some of my friends how they are addressed. Several insist on being "Mr." to their sons-in-law.

"I guess it's because I'm not yet quite ready to forgive him for stealing my daughter," said one.

William C. Inman of Raleigh has almost convinced me I should be less sensitive about being addressed by my last name.

"When someone calls me Inman," he writes, "I am called upon to do my best and not dishonor our tribe. Bound up in the name are ties to the land, to responsibility to personal substance. One is more than just a 'Bill,' comprising a bag of bones and a hank of hair; one has relations that define one's place in life.

"When people address you as 'Snow,' you should be proud of the unadorned term that links you with the distant past and the infinite future and brings the force of your tribe behind you."

I'll buy that.

December 1993

He has meat in his suitcase

When I read John Welter's side-splitting piece in Atlantic Magazine I thought of all the graduating college seniors who, resumes in the mail, are praying for what most of us once took for granted: a job. Or at least an interview for a job.

Considering the current economic climate, some even may be grateful for the job John Welter writes about: selling meat door to door.

A housewife answers the door bell and Mr. Welter is thinking:

"I want to tell her about my degree in English, the loveliness of Emily Dickinson, my affinity for Mark Twain, but I feel compelled to discuss the raw meat in my suitcase."

In a way, the new crop of job seekers will be peddling their personalities and talents door to door much like a seller of beef. In many cases, when talent is hard to determine, personality carries the day. And being candid can't hurt.

One of our editors recently interviewed a young man from upstate New York. She found him totally captivating, refreshingly candid.

At one point, he looked her in the eye, smiled and said, "My wife told me to work on eye contact."

"Well, how are you doing?"

"Pretty good, I guess. Eye contact isn't easy."

Later on, he smiled weakly and said, "Well, it's time to drop a name on you."

"Well, go ahead and drop it."

He mentioned a prominent editor whose newspaper has collected Pulitzer Prizes like teenage girls used to collect add-a-beads.

"Well, just how well do you know Gene?" our editor asked.

"My wife and his daughter are best friends."

"How well does Gene know your work?"

Making a tiny circle of his thumb and index figure, he said, with a sigh, "He knows far more about my table manners than he does my work."

I suggested she hire him immediately, if for nothing else than that rare ability among journalists not to take one's self too seriously.

Parents have all kinds of advice for their college grads. Most is rarely heeded. A couple of years ago, I tried to tell my youngest that, contrary to what the university career-counseling office said, she didn't have to wear a black suit. Navy would do just as well, especially since we had just bought her an expensive navy suit. But black it had to be.

During one memorable interview, and already as uptight as a violin string, she was totally unprepared for the interviewing editor's anger.

"I hate to be wasting my time interviewing you," he said bitterly. "I'd really like to hire somebody with three years' experience. But your type is all my budget will permit."

"Well, to tell you the truth," my daughter replied candidly, "I'd rather be interviewing for the New York Times, but you're the best I can do. I guess we both have to face reality and make the best of it."

"That's one job you've lost," I stormed when she related the incident.

I was wrong. She got the job. The navy suit had nothing to do with it.

I once concluded an interview by asking the job applicant if there was anything else he wanted to tell me about himself.

"Well, there is one thing about me that's unlike any other applicant you've ever interviewed," he said confidently.

"And what's that?"

"I have twice impregnated a priest."

He was married to an Episcopal priest and was the father of two children.

Good luck to you young job seekers. Dress neatly, yes, including shoes and socks. But relax and be yourself.

Be as honest and above-board as John Welter was when he said to the woman who answered the door bell, "Good morning, ma'am. We've killed some cows and I have them in my suitcase for you."

April 1992

You go there; she takes you in

When I was last in the foothills, I read in the Mount Airy News a touching story about a boy who had been mowing a field near his home and accidentally mowed over a rabbit burrow.

The mother rabbit was killed, leaving behind five tiny fluffs of fur that the lad took home and placed in a box in the kitchen.

As fate would have it, the family cat had recently given birth to a couple of kittens that had died. Within an hour, the cat jumped into the box, started licking the baby bunnies and immediately and irrevocably claimed them as her own.

According to the report, she is an excellent mother.

In all of God's creatures, no passion is more powerful or moving than the mothering instinct. And most mothers will tell you that giving birth is the easiest part of the parenting trip.

Since I have been semi-retired and trying to help out at home, my appreciation of the mother role has soared.

If I had had the responsibility of running a house, picking up the children's clothes, as well as the pieces of their lives, smearing all those peanut butter and jelly sandwiches, planning and executing three meals a day and teaching school, I would have jumped off the nearest bridge and considered myself lucky.

I know a few single fathers who have done a marvelous job substituting as Mom. But the basic instincts of caring, sacrifice and patience seem to be far less pronounced in most men.

It is Mom, not Dad, that children scream for during their midnight nightmares. On the battlefield, the dying cry out for mother. On TV, at the football games, the signs read "Hi Mom!" never "Hi Dad!"

Most mothers will tell you that it's not the physical exertion that takes its toll as much as it is the never-ending emotional drain of dealing with and loving children.

Even when it's time to let go and put down a part of the burden, mothers undergo a special sort of suffering.

I was reminded of that over the weekend when, as I was cleaning up the storage house, I came across the weather-beaten plywood door to the tree house that long ago disappeared from the lower limbs of a tree.

The door, high on my wife's sacred "not to be thrown out list," is her reminder of that far away and perhaps happier time when a mother had some control over her children's destiny.

I have come across an Erma Bombeck column a friend mailed to me some time ago. It expresses every mother's innate desire to shield her children from the hardships and disappointments that many of us proudly claim made us better than we might have been.

"We told them how we took eight years to pay off a secondhand shag rug, how we were married for five years before we owned a car. We made them sick they missed the Depression," she writes.

But she then echoes every mother's feeling:

"I don't want them to sell velvet pictures from door-to-door. I don't want them to buy gasoline $2 at a time. I don't want them to eat cold tacos from a doggy bag for breakfast.

"I don't want them to sell their bicycles and records to pay the rent. I don't want them to sleep cold and wear old.

"I want the birth without the pain. I want the pride without the loneliness. I want the success without the sacrifice."

And so it is.

In Robert Frost's "The Death of the Hired Man," there is the line, "Home is the place where, when you have to go there, they have to take you in."

Kids of all ages know that when the going gets rough, "mother" is a place where, when you have to go there, she has to take you in.

May 1992

Living with LBJ a class act

I never liked President Lyndon Johnson. It wasn't so much because of the Vietnam War. Nor the ruthless, clawing style that characterized his personal and political life.

When I saw him on TV, lifting his hounds "Him" and "Her" by their ears, I knew he had problems. A man who will do that to a dog might well do the same or worse to his wife.

But Lady Bird's was a class act. My admiration is borne out by an anecdote in a book I am now enjoying, "No News, Send Rumors," by Stephen Bates (St. Martin's Press, New York.)

This collection of American journalism anecdotes is chock full of true, often amusing confrontations between the press and the people they cover, from Oval Office to the bedrooms of the rich and famous.

When LBJ was running for re-election to the Senate, Dan Rather, a brash young newspaper reporter, hitched a ride out to the ranch for a news conference.

When the candidate didn't show up on time, young Rather concluded the whole thing was a publicity ruse. He sneaked inside the house to call his boss and tell him so.

Lyndon caught him red-handed, grabbed the phone out of Rather's hand and yelled into it, "This is Lyndon Johnson. I don't know who the hell you are, and I damned well don't know who this rude pissant is. But I can tell you this, I'm throwing his a— out."

Young Rather fled from the house and was racing down the road when he was overtaken by a white Lincoln Continental.

Lady Bird leaned out. "Whatever he said," she shouted, "he didn't mean anything by it, honey. It's just his way."

She then drove Rather back to the ranch.

I well remember feisty President Harry Truman's furious reaction to Washington Post critic Paul Hume's unfavorable review of daughter Margaret's singing debut.

"You sound like a frustrated old man who never made a success, an eight-ulcer man on a four-ulcer job and all four ulcers working," the president wrote. "I never met you, but if I do you'll need a new nose and a supporter below."

The White House can be vindictive. When Post reporter Judith Martin, now "Miss Manners," described Tricia Nixon as "a 24-year-old woman dressed like an ice-cream cone who can give neatness and cleanliness a bad name," she was banned from Tricia's wedding.

Traditionally, the White House press corps has been about as popular with presidents as a social disease.

Jimmy Carter called them "a bunch of prima donnas."

Thinking the mike had been turned off, after reporters had given him a hard time during a news conference, even easygoing President Reagan once muttered, "Sons of bitches!"

Mr. Bates' entertaining collection runs the gamut of past and present and a wealth of well-known personalities.

I have always wanted to know the identity of "Deep Throat," the source who brought those hot Watergate tips to Bob Woodward and Carl Bernstein in a post-midnight rendezvous at a D.C. parking garage.

But Bernstein never identified "Deep Throat" — not even to Nora Ephron, then his wife, who, he says, used to ask him.

"I had the good sense not to tell her."

The press — to its credit — has never aspired to winning popularity contests.

Donald Jones, an ombudsman for the Kansas City Star and Times, put it succinctly when he said, "You get a quart of sour milk at your local grocery store, you take it back to the checkout counter and say this milk is sour and the guy will say to you either, 'Get a new quart' or 'Here's your money back.'

"The equivalent of taking a quart of sour milk back to a newspaper is you're lucky if they don't pour it on your head."

We should remember the important distinction between journalism and milk. In the former, a popular press is not to be desired.

The public shouldn't want a watchdog hooked on sleeping pills.

February 1991

And oh, it gave a lovely light

You have your own short list of people you think God should have let live forever. William Bobbitt, the retired state Supreme Court chief justice, was near the top of mine.

Judge Bobbitt, who died this week, enriched the lives of so many of us with his wit, almost infinite wisdom and unfailing good manners that we feel something of great value has been taken from us. He came awfully close to being the complete man.

Also, this gently radiant man was a part of what was perhaps the most beautiful friendship I have ever witnessed.

I came to know him through Chief Justice Susie Sharp — the other half of that unique relationship — when I was a young reporter on The Raleigh Times.

Editor Herb O'Keef strolled up to my desk one morning to say that the town was atwitter with rumors that the two judges were about to wed.

"Call Judge Sharp and see if there is any truth to it," he instructed.

I almost rebelled. You just can't call up a Supreme Court justice at home and ask whether she was going to marry the chief justice. You could be sent to jail for contempt for something like that.

But because I myself was about to be married, it was no time to be out of a job. So I rang up Her Honor, who got out of the bathtub to answer the phone.

She was graciousness itself.

"No," she said, with a chuckle in her voice, "We're just good friends." She had long ago chosen law over marriage.

Popular, attractive, universally respected, the two were always in great demand: at the Kenan Stadium guest box, at the Executive Mansion, at most major public functions. Theirs was a class act, above reproach in every way.

My friendship with the two ripened after their retirement, when we would meet each Wednesday at First Presbyterian Church for midday lunch and worship service.

Both possessed a rich repertoire of wonderful stories, human dramas played out before them in courtrooms from Manteo to Murphy. Each Wednesday, I would hurry back to the office and enter the choice anecdotes into my computer. I entertained the idea of a book on their careers.

But the computer crashed one day during a summer thunderstorm, and my material was lost forever.

When I lamented the tragic loss to Judge Bobbitt, he said, his eyes twinkling, "Oh, don't worry, A.C., I tend to repeat myself."

Actually, he didn't. His keen mind was clear, his wit intact, until the day he died.

Humor was one of Judge Bobbitt's many hallmarks. One day he came to lunch directly from the Justice Building, where he had attended the unveiling of a portrait of a deceased member of the court. A justice has to die before his or her portrait can be hung.

During the ceremony, an admirer whispered, "Judge Bobbitt, I can't wait until they hang your portrait up there."

The two inseparable friends ate most of their meals together: breakfast at The Mecca, lunch at Hudson Belk and dinner at Balentines or the K&W. Occasionally, she cooked for him.

They both recalled with smiles the time Judge Bobbitt became ill in the middle of the night and rang up Judge Sharp.

"Judge," he said. "How do you feel?"

"Just fine, Judge. Until you woke me up. Why are you calling me at this hour?"

"I'm sick," he said. "Very sick. And I thought if you were sick, too, it might be that salmon souffle you served for dinner."

At the hospital the problem was traced to the judge's gallbladder, not the salmon souffle.

But that one night left a lasting scar on Judge Sharp's vanity, who always went about dressed as if she had stepped out of a fashion show. But in her concern for her good friend, she had not even bothered to comb her hair or put on makeup before transporting him to the hospital.

As the two stepped off the elevator, they were met by the doctor, who took one look at the usually chic Judge Sharp and wise-cracked, "Judge where did you park your broom?"

She never got over that night.

The candle of Judge Bobbitt's life burned brightly for almost 92 years before it flickered out. Throughout the years, as the poet said, it gave "a lovely light." And still does.

October 3, 1992

Guilt on back of the bus

The UNC Tar Heels' failure to bring home this year's NCAA championship found armchair coaches agog with answers.

"Dissension," said one. "I think this business of having the freshmen carry the upperclassmen's bags had as much to do with it as anything," said one die-hard fan. "That's a humiliating practice the Dean ought to drop. In fact, it smacks of racism."

Racism?

"Yeah," he said, citing freshman Rasheed Wallace's "I ain't gonna do it next year" comment during the tournament.

"If I were a superstar freshman and had to carry the bag of a senior who had maybe scored six points all year, I'd resent it, especially if I were black and the senior was white," he said.

But, as is often the case, rumor is more rancid than fact. Actually, the players don't carry each other's bags. The only bags the freshmen occasionally carry are equipment bags.

Today's perceived racism is so much more subtle than the hard-core variety I grew up with that it's sometimes difficult to discern. Many of us knew it firsthand, in all its incredible ugliness.

Few black families lived in the foothills. The black person we knew best was Sam, a wonderful extrovert who worked at the flour mill. Everybody professed great affection for Sam, but I never heard of anyone taking Sam home to dinner.

Memories of the mental cruelty we imposed on our fellow human beings in a segregated society came rushing back this week as I read columnist Art Buchwald's memoirs, "Leaving Home."

In one chapter, Art tells about riding the bus from Raleigh to Yemassee, S.C., on his way to Parris Island.

He had just joined the Marines, impulsively, and partly to spite his girlfriend at Woman's College in Greensboro.

"An elderly black lady with a tattered suitcase stood leaning over me. I got up to give her my seat, which she refused. The bus driver, who was watching in the mirror, stopped the bus.

"He came back to where I was standing and said, 'You sit back in your seat, you stupid son-of-a-bitch, or I'll throw you off this bus.'

"Then he did something weird. He apologized to the lady for my rudeness.

"The lady moved farther back so she wouldn't be standing near me. For her I was trouble."

Years later, Buchwald still remembers that little old lady on the bus "and how I had failed her."

A Jew who grew up in New York, Art could easily recognize the face of prejudice at its worst.

But I know a Southern boy who has felt that same sort of guilt for things not done and said in the long ago. As a youth, and even later, I felt similar compassion, but did very little to show it.

Oh, yes, there was an occasional exception, such as when an older brother visiting us in Raleigh used the six-letter word and I told him that if I heard it again I would have to ask him to leave.

As a reporter, my beat took me daily past the "White" and "Colored" water fountains on the Wake County courthouse lawn.

Even then I pondered how such a thing could be in the middle of the 20th century. You see, Raleigh had no Miss Jane Pittman to confront those water fountains and in one shining moment inspire us with her courage and shame us for our inhumanity.

While covering the lunch counter sit-ins at Raleigh's downtown Walgreen's and Woolworth's, I was repulsed by the rednecks pacing the sidewalk outside and bouncing baseball bats off the pavement.

Inwardly, I cheered the courageous young men and women perched on the lunch counter stools, as editor Herb O'Keef publicly applauded them on the Raleigh Times editorial page.

But I never had the guts to hop up there with them. I excused myself under the cloak of "professional objectivity."

The races have made great strides in learning how to live together as equals. I knew we had turned the corner when one day an elderly black woman wandered into a luncheonette and timidly asked the girl behind the counter, "Do you serve Colored here?" The girl replied, "Colored what?"

"Schindler's List," the monumental Oscar-sweeping movie depicting the horrible extremes of prejudice and hate, should surely leave Germans, young and old, forever saying, "I'm sorry."

Yet many of us stand guilty of a similar crime. I like to think that most of us share Buchwald's sense of remorse as we look back on that charade of "separate but equal" in the South.

March 1994

She has 'painful gas'

There's a radio commercial I find particularly disconcerting.
"My, your skin looks so shining," he says.
"Thank you," she says demurely.
"And your hair is so shining," he adds. They speak in such dulcet tones you'd think they are about to fall in bed.
So what's the product? I'm wondering.
Latex paint? Not likely.
A shining new shampoo?
Perhaps a skin cream that has just come on the market?
None of the above. It's a water-softener. Yeah, water-softener.

Advertising has come a long way since those uncomplicated Burma Shave signs sprouted beside the cornfields along rural highways back in the '30s and '40s, providing entertainment for bored kids on the back seat of the family car.

Although they would never have passed the poetry test for iambic pentameter, those little rhymes not only amused motorists but also dished out good common sense. The earliest verses from the late '20s were directed at hairy men:

He played a sax
Had no B.O.
But his whiskers scratched
So she let him go.

During World War II, Burma Shave also went to war. GIs on the road to the battle front in Italy passed one that read:

A GI Joe
From Venafro
Passed on a curve
Now he's
Six feet below.

These ads were written to be read in only three seconds from a car moving at 35 miles per hour. They and the shave cream company fell on bad times after World War II, partly because people were driving too fast to read the signs. They were all down by 1965.

Fortunes have been made in advertising. And still are. I guess that the popularity of the "mash box," as my children used to call the remote control button, surely has reduced TV ads' actual listening audience.

Although some ads are extremely clever, I watch very few. I'm vulnerable to those high-class Hallmark commercials or to ones featuring children, such as the one with the baby descending from heaven in an automobile tire.

I would never buy a car because of what is said or pictured on the screen. I switched to my present toothpaste after I read reliable research on the paste most likely to reduce cavities, not because some commercial promised to give me a grin that makes me irresistible to the opposite sex.

Sometimes I engaged in a little game in which I turn off the sound and try to guess the product.

Suddenly, a good-looking brunette glides across the screen. As the poet said, she walks in beauty. She has bedroom eyes and is dressed as exquisitely as a model on a Mademoiselle cover.

"Toothpaste?" I say to my wife.

"No, Estee Lauder," she guesses.

"Depends!" I offer. "It's Depends."

"No, it's June Allyson who does Depends."

She's right. It took me some time to accept the idea that my heartthrob of long ago is now selling diapers for adults.

To find the answer, I press the sound button.

"I have painful gas," the beautiful woman sighs.

The only ad I remember from childhood was the Bull Durham smoking tobacco posters plastered on tobacco barns and packhouses throughout rural North Carolina.

The poster featured a well-endowed bull pawing the ground.

We didn't have graffiti back then. But on poster after poster, somebody, probably teenage farm boys, had gone to the trouble to climb a ladder and use a crayon to draw attention to the animal's impressive underpinning.

One of the most delightful TV ads in recent history was Duke basketball coach Mike Krzyzewski's Final Four promotion.

Eddie Johnson, the "Yes, I am!" boy in the beer commercial, tells a limo driver he's Coach K, only to discover later that the limo driver is the real Coach K.

It was an ad for the season, and for all ages.

Elizabeth Stevens, of Garner, who has turned 4, greeted her dad at breakfast one morning.

"Ask me if I'm going to eat my cereal, Daddy," she said.

"OK, Elizabeth, are you going to eat your cereal?"

"Yes-I-am,' she grinned.

Yes, I consider my "mash box" one of life's most enriching inventions, even though when a good-looking woman appears on the muted screen, I can't help wondering if she has painful gas.

May 1994

'Streaking' without style

Ah, the lads in Lewis have let me down.
A former resident of Lewis Dorm at Chapel Hill, I have long kept up with the changes and trends there.
I have visited the dorm from time to time, occasionally stopping in at my old second floor room to chat with those who currently occupy what once was my tiny piece of Paradise.

But it's a bit embarrassing to a Lewis alumnus that the dorm's present residents seem to have made streaking their number one project at a time when streaking is no longer a competitive sport and indeed is totally out of vogue.

In my day, the campus had an occasional streaker. But back then, streaking had class. A streaker streaked bare from top to toe, unlike the Lewis lads who wear masks and streak with undershorts in hand, resembling Lone Rangers escaping from an early morning fire.

Also, in my day, streakers streaked solo, with the eyes of Texas upon you, so to speak.

Now the bare-tailed boys from Lewis streak in packs, which, like most mob action, is downright chicken.

If Lewis really wants to make a macho statement, the men should streak in winter, for heaven's sake.

Streaking in 32 degrees or below, with sleet or snow on the ground requires real commitment — not to mention showmanship.

And masks. Why masks? If you've got the goods to advertise, why not get credit? Nobody advertises in this newspaper without including the firm name. Streaking with a face mask reminds me of the story of three British clergymen who, during a summer retreat, liked to take morning walks in the nude by an isolated lake.

One morning they were surprised en route by a group of women out on a picnic. Two of the men instinctively covered their nakedness with their hands, while the third covered his face.

Moments later, one of his curious companions remarked, "Reverend, why did you cover your face when we met those women back there?"

"It all depends on how one is recognized," mused the minister.

On the college campus, streaking is as old as flunking. A friend of mine remembers a time back in the 1970s when his son streaked at N.C. State, where his daughter also was enrolled.

As the small contingent of nudes trotted triumphantly around the corner of one of the coed dorms, the daughter shrieked, "There goes my brother! Just wait 'til I tell Daddy!"

The news article about Lewis Dorm's streakers said they sing as they streak. What do they sing? If anyone has written music for streaking, I haven't heard of it. But the possibilities are limitless.

When I was a kid in Sunday school at Charity Baptist Church, we sometimes sang a little song called, "This little light of mine, I'm gonna let it shine." That might be appropriate.

I really don't understand the university's pious position on streaking. Here we have Dean Fred Schroeder counseling the boys that "what was once considered a harmless 'boy's game' is no longer acceptable in this campus community."

Say again? Isn't this the same campus that for years has permitted all-night dorm visitation between the sexes?

Isn't this the Berkeley of the South that opened the state's first coed dorms, where residents can streak from floor to floor, up and down the halls, or in their lady's chamber?

It's not that I don't approve the dean's efforts. I say good luck and Godspeed.

But trying to restore chastity to today's college campus seems about as hopeless as attempting a 60-yard field goal when your team is trailing 76-0.

The problem, it seems to me, is that today's college students have run out of causes. They are flailing at windmills while hurricanes blow all about.

For example, a group of Carolina students recently launched a protest against the $100 a year tuition increase passed by the legislature. Talk about a straw man!

That comes to $50 a semester, about what the average Carolina man spends in two weeks on beer, pizza and parking tickets. Less than a pair of tickets to the Rolling Stones.

And a couple of weeks ago, a covey of Carolina coeds marched on The Daily Tar Heel, demanding that the business manager pull a Playboy ad.

What kind of a campus is this? Some of the coeds applaud passing streakers while others want to put their daily newspaper out of business by censoring Playboy ads?

It's true that today's students have no Vietnam War to protest. But we have wars aplenty: a war against drugs, a war against poverty, a war against smoking.

What are the soldiers in Lewis Dorm doing about these wars? They're streaking — with masks on, and carrying their Jockeys, just in case they're recognized.

It's enough to make an old Lewis alumnus want to cover his face with his hands.

September 1989

Saving safety pins and past

A longtime friend of mine is getting his papers together — the memorabilia of his life.

Dave's office walls are covered with commendations and awards. Scrapbooks and file folders bulging with life's personal mementoes. Letters from his father. Valentine and birthday cards with his kids' scrawled signatures. Photos that document his family's history.

Even the game ball and the football helmet his late, much-admired brother-in-law wore during the Gator Bowl game of an almost forgotten yesteryear lies in the corner, a reminder of fame's swift fleeting.

I behold his work with mingled relief and regret. I have saved so little from the past, no awards, no clothes except my Air Force uniform, very few letters.

With the exception of my dear departed Uncle Everett, my family is not a family of savers. Older relatives tell how during the Depression, he hoarded everything — pieces of strings, rusty nails, old horseshoes, etc.

They chuckle over the story of the lost safety pin. Uncle Everett had gone to the far side of the farm to clear new ground for a tobacco plant bed.

For his mid-morning snack, he had tucked a baked sweet potato into his jacket pocket, sealing the pocket with a safety pin. While removing his lunch at noon, he accidentally dropped the safety pin in the leaves.

After much fruitless searching, he stopped by a neighbor's on the way home and said to the woman of the house.

"I have lost a safety pin over in yonder woods. I left a little pile of rocks to mark the place. I want you to know that if any of you find it, you're welcome to keep it."

I suspect my aversion to accumulating life's souvenirs can be traced in part to a moment some years ago when I called upon a relative whose father had just died.

I found her in her father's bedroom closet, angrily hurling his clothes — old trousers, shirts and shoes — into a pile on the floor.

"Damn him!" she said, tears streaming down her face, "Look what a horrible mess he left for me to dispose of. All these old clothes! All these old memories!"

Unlike me, my wife cannot let go of anything. Before embarking on a plane trip, she inevitably admonishes me, "Now if something should happen to me, don't let anybody in the house until you have straightened up the downstairs closets."

And I inevitably reply, "But you can't postpone a funeral for a whole month."

But my efforts to bulldoze hers and the children's past are hopeless.

Not long ago, my daughter Katherine, preparing a toast for the prenuptial dinner of a friend from childhood, said wistfully "I wish I had kept those letters Beth McConnell wrote to me in junior high. But when I cleaned up my room the last time I was home. I finally put them in the trash."

My wife quietly left the room, returning shortly with the yellowed notes clutched triumphantly in her hand.

She had salvaged them from the big plastic bag of trash I had planned to put out for the garbage man but couldn't find.

We had a good chuckle over the childish notes:

Note: "I guess I do like Joel although I told you I did not. Joel makes me sick! Can you believe he would do that? Well if you think about it, I can believe he would do that."

Note: "Look at the way Catherine Averett smiles at Rick. Why does she do that when she knows I like him? Do you think he likes me? Does he know I like him? What should I do?"

Note: "I'm sorry I kicked you. I shouldn't have. But you shouldn't have blamed me for your not having your homework."

We are what we are. It's much easier to keep than to throw away. Perhaps there is a happy medium in which we can leave a few footprints in the sand without saving the entire desert.

I wish now I had settled for that middle ground.

March 1992

Preachers' kids hurt, too

One of my friends went home to visit his parents recently and hadn't been there long before his dad said, "Well, the preacher drove out yesterday to show us his new Cadillac."

"A Cadillac? Boy, you must pay your preacher well," the son said.

"Son, I don't pay the preacher anything. I pay the Lord."

"Well, the Lord pays the preacher well then," the son amended.

"It was a red Cadillac," the father added, almost wistfully.

"Well, I'm glad the Lord is doing well by the preacher," the son said. "Just be sure the Lord doesn't buy him two red Cadillacs."

I admire my friend's father. He isn't offended or jealous that his minister drives a handsome new car.

After all, the minister's outward sign of prosperity reflects how well the congregation is treating God's spokesman.

Yes, this sort of thing can get out of hand, as it did with evangelist Jim Bakker and others.

When a red Caddie graduates into gold doorknobs or platinum bathroom faucets, it's time to wonder what the Lord is up to.

There was a time, and I'm glad it's past, when ministers were treated like society's red-headed stepchildren.

Living in a glass bowl, they and their children, like Caesar's wife, had to be above reproach. They weren't expected to live as comfortably, certainly not more comfortably, than members of their flocks.

Ministers' children had it even tougher than the ministers.

They had to show up every time the church door cracked. They had to sweat out Dad's sermons, stay awake and refrain from squirming or looking bored, no matter how long he rambled on.

They couldn't smoke, cuss, drink, stay out late or make out on dates.

When I was in high school, the preacher's son was the handsomest boy in the class and took full advantage of it.

He had all the teachers clucking in disapproval over his flagrant hand-holding with the dentist's daughter.

"Imagine, the preacher's son!" someone would say, as if preachers' sons were born without hormones.

But Foy wasn't intimidated in the least. He married the girl and sired six children.

My compassion for children of the cloth is traceable, in part, to having shared from time to time the reminiscences of a good friend who is a Methodist minister's daughter.

While she is in no way bitter about her youth, she cannot forget some of the small hurts that haunted her childhood.

For one thing, Methodist ministers rarely knew where they would land next. They were God's nomads, at the mercy of the bishop. They couldn't even own much of anything, since most were provided furnished parsonages.

"I remember that Daddy did buy for him and mother a good set of mattress and springs that we hauled from town to town," my friend recalled. "But we usually left the rest behind, moving on to whatever accommodations the new congregation could afford or felt inclined to provide."

The mother was a lovely, saintly woman. I knew her personally. She never complained — about anything.

My friend recalls that one of the very few times she saw her mother cry was when she came home from a meeting of Women's Missionary Society, which was in charge of the parsonage. Her mother had submitted a request for a chest of drawers for the bedroom.

A prominent woman in the community had stood up at the meeting and said haughtily, "What they have is good enough for them!"

A few days later, the apparently conscience-stricken dowager showed up at the preacher's house, bearing two live chickens as tokens of apology.

In the "olden days," preachers' wives made most of the children's clothes.

But one Easter, this mother pulled together enough "egg money," to get "store-bought" coats for her two little girls. The children were ecstatic, even though their mother urged them not to mention the coats at church.

"We didn't get a chance to," my friend recalls. "When we walked into Sunday school, we were greeted by one of my best friends — the daughter of perhaps the richest man in town.

"Her mouth dropped open in astonishment, and she angrily blurted at the top of her voice, 'Look! They have on new coats!'"

Things have changed for the better for the clergy.

Ministers' families in general have more control over their destinies, even though they will always live in glass houses.

But at least the kids no longer have to go to great lengths to prove to their peers that they aren't really as pure as they are expected to be.

And if God wants to give one of his deserving servants a new Cadillac — or even a BMW — well, that's OK, too.

Isn't it about time?

March 1994

When angels 'tinkle' on stage

A few days before Christmas, an attractive young woman came up to me at a bookstore and flattered me by saying our chance acquaintance was the nicest thing that had happened to her all day.

But then it hadn't been a particularly good day. She had been shopping for six hours while her husband was at home caring for their 6-year-old son who had a fever of 101. And there also was a 3-year-old.

A music teacher in the elementary grades, she had just directed the school's Christmas pageant the night before.

"Wouldn't you know it? One of the little angels tinkled right there on the stage," she sighed. "And then today, my doctor calls to say, 'Yes, you really are pregnant.'"

But as she went merrily down the mall, I knew that she would prevail. She realized that life itself is incredibly like a play that does not always go according to script.

We are again in the midst of the pageant season. And kids being kids, I hold my breath along with the pageant directors.

A First Baptist Church member recalls a memorable Christmas pageant at the church several years ago.

Two youngsters had tried out for the role of Joseph. The loser did not accept his lesser role as the innkeeper very gracefully. He brooded over revenge.

During the pageant, when Joseph came with Mary to ask for a room at the inn, the offended innkeeper, instead of following the well-known script and turning the couple away, said, cheerfully, "Oh, come on in, we got lots of room!"

However, the pageant director's wisdom in handing out the roles was borne out by the spontaneous response from the young Joseph.

"No way! Do you think I would let my wife sleep in a dump like this?"

A Sunday or so ago, on Channel 4, I happened to catch Dr. Leo Buscaglia, the popular psychologist. He was describing the Christmas pageant he directed on his first job as an elementary school teacher.

He had decided his production would be different. The kids would deliver the lines spontaneously. No set script, no tired old routines.

For Joseph, he chose a kid named Matthew, the biggest boy in the class — athletic, hyper, the nonreader.

Dr. B pointed out that when the principal visits your classroom, this is the kid you rush over to put your arms around because that's the only way you're going to know where he is.

On the night of the unorthodox pageant, Mary and Joseph are leaning against each other, asleep, when the angel appears and quietly places the baby Jesus at Mary's feet.

Mary stirs. Joseph slowly opens his eyes and, seeing the baby, cries, "Hey Mary! Look what you had during the night!"

There was a long, awful silence before the audience erupted with laughter and applause.

It was the best pageant ever, and nonreader Matthew, exhilarated by his successful performance, rushed up afterward and said, "Mr. B., I'm not going to be a basketball player after all! I'm going to be an actor!"

Dr. Buscaglia had good advice for this hectic season of the year. Laugh a lot.

"At Christmas, if you have turkey and your contrary sister-in-law says 'I want a goose!' give her a goose! But be happy!"

Each family has its own Christmas pageant. Some are relaxed, others stressful. Few go according to script.

Keep in mind what is important. Strip away the tinsel of the season. Put aside the imaginary hurts and slights.

Listen for church bells on a clear night. Study the stars, and seek out the bright one. Reach for someone to hug.

Send up a prayer for those in a Saudi desert where the stars seem awfully close but where Christmas is awfully far away.

For each of you, a happy holiday.

December 1990

The nuttiest day of the year

During the Super Bowl rout of Buffalo by the Dallas Cowboys, I worried for the wives of Bills' fans.

A recent news story quoted a survey that said wife beatings soar on Super Bowl Sunday. Although the "survey" later turned out to be a hoax aimed at further hyping the Super Bowl game, I suspect there might be a grain of truth in the assumption.

In my own circle of acquaintances, I don't think there is a man who would stoop to wife battering, either as a practiced sport or just on impulse. But if he did, there isn't a wife in my circle of acquaintances who would let him get away with it.

In fact, two days before the Super Bowl, a friend of mine was driving along Oberlin Road when she saw a woman beating the daylights out of a man who was trying desperately to cover his head with his coat to ward off her blows.

When another man came to his rescue, she turned on him with equal enthusiasm and put both males to flight.

I'm sure this is a rare exception to the spouse abuse trend, which finds the male far more prone to violence than the female.

On that same weekend, as Wake Forest was dismantling the Tar Heels on the basketball court, I found my irritation level soaring.

"Will you ever in your life be able to accept the fact that your team can't win every time?" my wife asked in response to my bursts of outrage and moans of disgust.

"No," I said sadly. "I thought I could. I thought I was over it. But I probably never will be."

Still, I see myself as the Pharisee in the Bible who, overhearing the sinner confessing his sins, says sanctimoniously, "God, I thank thee that I am not like other men."

In other words, I don't think I'm nearly as sick as those fans who bash their women as a part of the high they get from watching athletic violence on TV.

In a magnificent article on the national sickness, Washington Post writer Cal Fussman once wrote, "Sports is the clean white bandage we have placed over a festering abscess at the core of this country. Why should we be surprised when a little pus seeps?"

How true. The Super Bowl with all its excess is only the epitome of a widespread problem that begins in Pee Wee and Little League.

When beer companies pay $750,000 for a half-minute commercial, when adults pay $425 for the 1963 baseball card of Pete Rose, when

Dwight Gooden, returning to Shea Stadium after admitting to drug abuse, is given a standing ovation by 50,000 fans, something is sick out there, folks.

The sickness is further underscored when the network sacrifices one of those $750,000 half-minute spots to say, in effect, to the men watching, "Hey guys, if you don't like the way this thing ends, please don't give your 'old lady' a shiner. It's bad for the image."

Sports is the panacea for the frustrations of life.

As Fussman says, the sports fan "uses his team for a fraudulent sense of community; a close game as a substitute for the lack of tension in his life; a victory as salve for his own defeats.

"Reggie Jackson once said that hitting a home run is better than having sex. That may be. The problem is, for many Americans, watching a Reggie Jackson hit a home run is better than having sex."

The Super Bowl holds little interest for me unless the Redskins are in it. So at halftime, I put away the pizza and popcorn and left the place where a few of us had congregated.

Such a trickle of traffic along my usually congested route home had me puzzled until I remembered how Fussman ended his piece:

"On a Sunday in late January, a day when 122 million Americans simultaneously sat, embalmed, in front of television sets, I took a walk through streets and over lawns, listening to the blades of grass crunch under my feet, looking into the gray sky, the horizon littered with antennas. A dog howled in the distance. On and on I walked through the empty streets. Nowhere was there a sign of human life."

I am beyond explaining the mania of millions of sports fans, including my own ridiculous reactions to a win or loss.

In fact, I'm inclined to agree with someone who said, "There's nothing wrong with sports that getting rid of sports fans wouldn't cure."

January 1994

'So, what's a honeymoon?'

We were standing around after the wedding, and I must have mentioned something about honeymoons, perhaps where I went on my own honeymoon. I'm not sure.

Anyway, a young man who, I understand, enjoys one of those live-in relationships, asked with a wry smile, "What's a honeymoon, anyway?"

"I don't know what it is now," I remember saying. "I only know what it used to be."

Webster says the term comes from the French and is based on the idea that the first month of marriage is the sweetest. It is defined as "a period of unusual harmony immediately following marriage."

I'm here to tell you that in my day there was considerably more excitement, anticipation and, yes, apprehension in a honeymoon than Mr. Webster apparently knew about. To me, harmony was just a small town in Iredell County.

For most women, a honeymoon was an exciting, if not traumatic, experience.

Few brides, in the language of the Bible, "knew" a man before the wedding night. And even for grooms who might have tinkered around with premarital passion, the honeymoon was not just a ho-hum "period of harmony."

As a friend said, "Just realizing that you were going to be able to sleep with someone special for the rest of your life would give even the most macho man food for thought."

During the week I took off from work prior to my wedding, I spent the nights gulping tranquilizers and the days washing my Carolina blue and white retractable hardtop convertible.

Garrison Keillor, in "We Are Still Married," addresses the male's anxiety in the most delightful way.

In preparation for his wedding night, Keillor says he "stood at the edge of Riverside Park above the river and attempted to make outbursts of sexual passion. Loud ones like Tarzan, soft sighs, grunts, some growling. I tried yipping and wahooing, even something sort of like yodeling.

"Then it hit me: What if sex for her and me turned out to be nothing to yip and wahoo about, but a series of small and sort of interesting events like a checkers match in the course of which you'd say, 'Are you having a good time?' or 'As long as I'm up, can I get you anything?'

"I was a Minnesota guy and we are no great lovers. Minnesotans make love once a month, on the 15th, and when it's over and done with they don't whoop and holler or smoke a cigarette and listen to Bach. They get up and brush their teeth. Then they go to bed. When a Minnesotan sleeps with someone, normally he sleeps."

Oh, sure, there's more to a honeymoon than raw passion. Or used to be. You learned things about each other you never knew before, things like which side of the bed your mate likes to sleep on, what brand of toothpaste he or she brings to the marriage.

Many a bride might never have gone into the marriage had she known that the groom snored like a cavefull of bears, or that he insisted on hogging two-thirds of the bed.

Ah, yes, you say, that's the advantage of living together before marriage. You iron out all the problems beforehand and there are no surprises.

I concede the point. But try to understand that many of us feel like Meg Greenfield, in a June 22 Newsweek column on Dan Quayle and "family values":

'In this, the month of June 1992, it is a fact still astonishing to some of us old fogies that a lot of brides-to-be of all political persuasions and parties climb out of the bed they have shared with their boyfriends for five years, put on a white wedding dress and march down a church aisle to be married to said boyfriend."

If I ever see that young man again I'm going to ask him what he did on his honeymoon. It's possible that he just slept. The way a man from Minnesota sleeps.

July 1992

A different hen each time

When President Bush collapsed during the state dinner in Tokyo and upchucked under the table, my heart went out to him. Undoubtedly, it was his most embarrassing moment.

But I liked his rejoinder: "I just wanted to get a little attention."

It reminded me of Ronald Reagan's comment as he was going into surgery after the assassination attempt on his life.

Looking up at the doctors he said, "Please assure me that you are all Republicans."

To which one of the doctors responded, "Today, we are all good Republicans, Mr. President."

Good leadership requires a strong sense of humor. It humanizes humans who, when they assume high offices, tend to become immortal in their own mind.

After reading "Presidential Anecdotes," an entertaining volume by Paul E. Boler Jr., I realize that few American presidents have been totally void of wit.

Even dry, colorless Calvin Coolidge had his moments. Perhaps the best remembered one occurred during a tour of an Iowa poultry farm.

Mrs. Coolidge, walking ahead of the president, happened to see a rooster performing his duties and asked how many times a day it rose to the occasion.

"Dozens," the guide replied, to which Mrs. Coolidge quipped, "Tell that to the president."

Apparently someone did. When the president came along and saw the same rooster at work, he asked, "Is it always the same hen?"

"Oh, no," he was told. "A different hen each time."

"Tell that to Mrs. Coolidge," the president snapped.

Lyndon Johnson was one of our most abrasive and arrogant presidents. It is reported that that during a visit to the LBJ ranch, Germany's Ludwig Erhard said, "I understand you were born in a log cabin, Mr. President.

"No, Mr. Chancellor," replied Johnson, "I was born in a manger."

Johnson also was quick to anger, and his associates tread lightly around him. But press secretary Bill Moyers once dared bite back.

Moyers was saying grace at a White House luncheon when Johnson snapped, "Speak up, Bill, I can't hear a damned thing."

"I wasn't addressing you, Mr. President," Moyers replied softly.

Although, on TV, John F. Kennedy always seemed to have a twinkle in his heart, I can't recall many belly laughs at his expense.

Boler records that once, when Kennedy, then a congressman, parked in a "No Parking" zone, he remarked to a friend, "This is what Hamlet meant by 'the insolence of office.'"

Also, when a high school kid asked, "Mr. President, how did you become a war hero?" he replied, "They sank my boat."

One of President Reagan's friends sent him a clipping in which a California state senator charged that "illegitimate births to teenage mothers have increased alarmingly since Reagan has been in office."

"Thanks very much for the clipping," Reagan wrote back. "I have never felt so young and virile."

Gerald Ford, one of our most likable and lovable presidents, earned an undeserved reputation for clumsiness because of a couple of minor mishaps. Actually, he was very athletic.

But Ford possessed a Quayle-like penchant for putting his foot in his mouth. His most memorable faux pas: "If Lincoln were alive today, he'd roll over in his grave."

The necessity for humor in high office was well expressed on an engraved silver beer mug President Kennedy once gave to a friend:

There are three things which are real:
God, human folly and laughter.
The first two are beyond comprehension,
So we must do what we can with the third.

I'll say "Amen!" to that.

January 1992

On the sad side of lonesome

After 38 years, Tammy Faye is finally leaving her man. And leaving him behind bars.

"I'm so very lonely," she said. "And hurting."

She's hurting? What about him?

The same day that Tammy Faye told Jim it was finally over, my car radio was on and country singer Jim Reeves was telling how it really feels to be lonesome:

I'm just on the blue side of lonesome
Next door to the Heartbreak Hotel
In a tavern that's known as Three Teardrops
On a bar stool, not doing so well.

Now that's lonesome. We've all been on the blue side of lonesome. A survey of 3,000 Americans revealed that loneliness ranks ninth among Americans' 10 worst fears. Speaking in public still finishes first.

I usually undergo an attack of lonesome when my wife leaves town for a few days. Sure, I share the feeling of a friend who says, "I like structuring my own life from time to time without having to consider anyone else.

"I can read a book in silence. I can leave dishes in the sink. I can greet the dawn by myself, without having to tiptoe down the stairs to the kitchen or the porch." But that grows old in a hurry.

Undoubtedly, women also enjoy the same sense of freedom. Absence, short bursts of it, is good for a marriage. For women, it's one less egg to fry.

The last time I came home from an out-of-town trip I asked my wife if she didn't enjoy my absence.

"I don't want to hurt your feelings, but yes, I did," she said. "I enjoyed being responsible only for me, eating dinner at any hour I chose and not being accountable to another living soul for a few days."

As insurance against a wounded ego, she added, "But I don't think I could bear it if I thought you weren't ever coming back."

My worst siege of "lonesome" came when, at age 18, I was snatched from the bosom of my family and my beloved foothills by Uncle Sam and dumped on the hot sands of Biloxi, Miss., for basic training.

Exhausted after long days of drilling, calisthenics and verbal abuse at the hands of a sadistic drill sergeant, I would sit alone on the barracks steps at night, staring up the sky and thinking that those same stars, that same moon, were shining down on the folks back home. Did they miss me? Would I ever see them again? Talk about heartbreak hotel!

What parent has not left a child at camp, glancing back for one last look at the forlorn figure sitting on the footlocker, big brown eyes welling with tears, a small hand lifted in a halfhearted wave?

What wife has not insisted that the husband drive back to the camp next morning for one more goodbye, only to be turned back by dense fog on the narrow mountain road, leaving the first born behind to cope with her first — but but by no means last — major case of lonesome?

You don't have to be alone or out of the limelight to be lonely.

The late Judy Garland once complained, "If I'm such a legend, then why am I so lonely? If I'm such a legend, then why do I sit at home for hours staring at the damned telephone, hoping it's out of order, even calling the operator asking her if she's sure it's not out of order. Let me tell you, legends are all very well if you've got somebody around who loves you…"

Same song, last verse:

The floor has a carpet of sorrow
But no one can cry in the aisle.
And they say someone broke the bar mirror
With only a ghost of a smile.

I hear you hurting, Tammy Faye. But my heart goes out to Jim as he paces his "carpet of sorrow."

April 1992

Saluting "Big Pilot in the Sky"

My old Air Force outfit is having another reunion. I have never been to one. St. Louis in October? I'm not sure.

The newsletter announcing the get-together is not very cheerful. The editor, Gene Diamond, of Wheaton, Ill., warns that chances to renew old acquaintances are running out.

"We are losing too many of our comrades to the Big Pilot in the Sky," he notes.

As I read through the newsletter I noticed that all references to officers were capitalized — Officers — whereas enlisted man was always lowercased.

I do not remember Mr. Diamond, since he was not a member of my squadron. So when I rang him up for more information on the reunion, I couldn't resist asking, "Were you an officer?"

"Yes," he said proudly, "I'm a retired lieutenant colonel."

"I thought so by the way you capitalized the 'O' in officers."

Officers never quite get over being officers. Enlisted men, with memories like elephants, never quite get over some officers being officers.

I still remember a telephone call from an irate subscriber when I was editor of The Raleigh Times. I had always prided myself on my patience in handling complaints.

But this fellow just wouldn't be mollified. Finally, his arrogance overflowed.

"I'll have you know you're talking to a U.S. Army lieutenant colonel, retired!" he yelled, apparently expecting me, somehow, to salute over the telephone.

"That's no excuse for bad manners," I snapped. "You ought to be over it by now."

Of course not all lieutenant colonels retired are as boorish. I have some good friends who reached that rank, and higher. And the pilots in my squadron were smart enough not to throw their weight around — at least not overseas.

They soon learned that, one way or another, the enlisted men usually had the last word.

I remember when, out on the flight line in New Guinea, one of our tough young master sergeants stood at the edge of the jungle relieving himself. Along came a fuzz-faced captain, just over from the States, who drew himself up short and yelled, "Sergeant! Just what do you think you're doing?"

Without so much as glancing away from the job at hand, Master Sgt.

Swain replied cheerfully in the common vernacular, "P——, sir!" And that was that.

The newsletter listed a couple of fliers in my squadron who recently had joined the Great Pilot in the Sky. Flipping through my squadron yearbook — The Biscuit Bomber — I found them there, standing by their plane, smiling cockily. They were just kids, as we all were, certain that God would not let happen to us what he had let happen to so many others.

Do I really want to go back to puzzle over faces I would not recognize without name tags? Isn't it better to remember them as they were, as in A.E. Housman's "To an Athlete Dying Young," — lads who never wore their honors out, runners who did not outrun their fame, men whose name did not die before the man.

But why are we even tempted?

Matthew Broderick in Neil Simon's "Biloxi Blues" answered that question better than I when he said, "As I look back now, a lot of years later, I realize that my time in the Army was the happiest time of my life.

"God knows not because I liked the Army, and there sure was nothing to like about a war.

"I liked it for the most selfish reason of all, because I was young. We all were, me and Epstein and Wykowski, Selridge, Carney, Hennesey and even Sergeant Toomey. I didn't really like most of those guys then, but today I love every damn one of them. Life is weird, you know."

I doubt I will go to St. Louis, choosing instead to greet my Air Force buddies when I report to the Great Pilot in the Sky, who, I am convinced, will not require a salute from me.

I have a sneaky feeling He never went to OCS.

July, 1992

'Potatoe' no small potato

To think, this could be the year that the presidential election swings on which party is more grammatically correct.

Dan Quayle's "potatoe" and Bill Clinton's pronoun error — "Give Al Gore and I a chance" — are campaign issues.

Yup, it's back to basics.

Hallelujah!

To know where I'm coming from, you have to realize that in grade school I was usually the last kid chosen for the ballgame at recess. It was a toss-up between me and Tommy Spicer as to who struck out more consistently. Being chosen next to last made my day.

But the tables were turned every Friday afternoon when we had our spelling bee.

When the team captains picked their squads, it wasn't Abou Ben Adam's name that led all the rest. It was A.C. Snow's!

Of course the warm fuzzy was only temporary. Great spellers are not remembered or revered nearly as much as great hitters, great sprinters or fast drivers. The jock has always kicked sand in the egghead's eyes. And always will.

Many of you know what I mean.

My friend Mike Skube recalls how in the eighth grade, he wanted desperately to be named sports editor of the school newspaper, which was staffed primarily by girls.

Deeply interested in sports, but too small to play, Mike would sit in front of the TV and write up any number of big games, comparing his work with what the Associated Press wrote the next day.

"I thought I was a shoo-in," he recalls. "I was the only boy in the class who ever stood a chance of wresting a spelling bee title from one of the girls.

"But when it came to filling the mid-level vacancies, the girls showed they were girls after all. All the jocks got the good jobs, and the most strapping of them was ceremoniously named sports editor.

"I was crushed. The good Sister Mary Theresa, sensing my disappointment, put her arm on my shoulder and told me the job should have been mine. I thought so, too, and have ever since been doubtful of the woman's vote," said Mike, who went on to win a Pulitzer Prize while at The News & Observer.

In "One Writer's Beginning," Eudora Welty tells how she once disappointed her parents by not making 100 on a spelling test.

She missed one word — uncle. Her mother took it personally.

"You mean, you couldn't spell uncle, when you've got those five perfectly splendid uncles in West Virginia? What would they say to that?"

Prowess in spelling no longer commands pride. When a boy dreams of being another Michael Jordan or even the CEO of IBM with a secretary, he's not apt to stay after school to learn how to spell potato.

Even if he doesn't have a smart secretary, he'll surely have a smart computer. Like mine.

Press the "spell" button and my Coyote will swiftly scan this column and cough up all the misspelled words.

But ah, there's a catch. As the Wall Street Journal noted recently, computer spell checkers can make sure words are spelled correctly. But few can guarantee they're used correctly.

Consider this poem circulated at Coastal Corp. in Houston:

I have a spelling checker.
It comes with my PC.
It plainly marks four my revue
Mistake I cannot see.
I've run this poem threw it,
I'm sure you're please too no.
It's letter perfect in it's weigh
My checker tolled me sew.

You will note that every word is spelled correctly, but that those eight lines contain no fewer than 12 usage errors.

Yes, if this campaign can give credence to good grammar it will have accomplished more than most. After all, spelling used to be one of those "family values" we're hearing so much about.

August 1992

They're always 'only 18'

From the deck of the carrier Independence parked in the Persian Gulf, Dan Rather introduced us to some of the crew. A burr-headed fighter pilot said yes, he felt fear in the pit of his stomach.

The camera focused fleetingly on a sailor reading "Red Badge of Courage," Stephen Crane's Civil War classic depicting in gory detail the horrors of war.

This is not a book to be read by boys going into battle.

Mr. Rather shoved the mike into the face of a shy young fellow and invited him to say something to the folks back home.

"Hi, Mom and Dad," he said.

The newsman waited, the mike still outstretched.

Waiting for what? A muttered "I love you, Mom" or a pleading "Tell me, Dad, what am I doing here?"

Neither came from the silent sailor. Young men just don't blurt out "I love you" or admit fear before the whole world and their peers. It isn't macho.

I heard sniffling and turned to see tears coursing down my wife's face.

"They're only 18!" she whispered, her voice breaking.

"They're always only 18," I explained. "I was only 18."

Next morning, at the cafe where I go for coffee, the perky young waitress I have come to know was worried. A recent enlistee in the National Guard, Michelle had come face to face with both her drill sergeant and the dark shadow of war.

Ah, the D.I. He is Mom, Dad, teacher, boss, God and the Devil all packaged into one, usually insensitive, frame.

On drill night, the D.I., standing eyeball to eyeball with her, had loudly ordered her to recite the third General Order. Disconcerted by his bulldog approach, she couldn't remember the third General Order. Or any General Order. All she could do was grin.

"Wipe that silly grin off your face!" the D.I. had yelled. "In combat, somebody's gonna shoot it off!"

The apprentice soldier resorted to tears.

Her story was almost a replay of a recent call from another young recruit who had failed to salute a second lieutenant. Hell hath no fury like a second lieutenant unsaluted.

"It was awful," she said. "He yelled and cussed. I explained that I didn't salute because I thought he was a warrant officer. Then he yelled and cussed even louder and threatened to have me do extra duty and a hundred push-ups.

"I finally burst into tears and told him I had only been in the Army five days. Then he was very apologetic and said, 'Now, now, soldier, don't cry, don't cry.'"

It's almost amusing, this coed army.

How does a tough-as-nails, mean-as-hell drill sergeant or an ego-swollen second lieutenant cope with soldiers who cry when they're cussed?

There is nothing funny about the Mideast standoff that has caused an anxiety crisis among thousands of youths who took the TV commercials seriously, and signed on to see the world, have a ball and a beau in every port.

As Michelle said, "When I enlisted, there was no crazy nut running around talking about a 'holy war.' And nobody said anything about mustard gas."

A Raleighite said he recently overheard a spoiled young man he knows echo a familiar refrain, "I'm not going to Saudi Arabia. I'll go to Canada first."

"For the good of the country, I sure hope so," the man had said under his breath.

When you hear about Saddam Hussein's well-trained, well-oiled million-man army, you think about the immature, fuzzy-faced youths assigned to defend America. You almost panic.

Then you remember that wars have always been fought by boys who overnight have had to become men. Somehow they get the job done.

Pray that none of these will have to prove their mettle with a red badge of courage. Buying oil with the blood of youth is bad business.

August 1990

In every frog a handsome prince

Harold came up to me in the snack bar. His eyes were on fire with anticipation. His lip curled sadistically. Harold is a serial killer — of animals.

"Just wanted you to know, I've bought new flashlight batteries. I've sharpened my gig. And I'm going out tonight to round up some of your little green friends."

Harold was going gigging. He gets turned on to what some call a sport by sharing the graphic details of the impending slaughter with me.

It's not that frogs are my thing. I can take 'em or leave 'em. And I've been gigging only once, drafted by an older brother when I was a kid.

My job was to carry the bag of frogs speared by my brother and a hard-drinking neighbor from the adjoining farm. That was enough.

But there must be something in the August air that sets off some people's lust for violence when it comes to frogs and the like.

The day after my encounter with Harold, a woman called WPTF's "Ask Your Neighbor" for advice on how to deal with the army of "toad frogs" that had encamped in her yard.

A moment later, a Johnston County woman asked in a no-holds-barred voice, "Does anyone have any snap-turtle recipes? We're going to wipe out those pesky turtles in our pond."

A response was not long in coming. A caller read from the "White Trash Cookbook" one of the most blood-curdling recipes I've ever heard.

You start by boiling the turtle alive. Then you scoop out the body, saving the shell, and add a wide-ranging variety of spices and stuff. The recipe includes a healthy shot of whiskey.

The liquor must help kill the taste and muster courage to eat the stuff, I thought as I drove along.

Frogs are peace-loving critters. I'm told there is a worldwide shortage of them, so many have been killed in traffic or murdered for their legs. At the supermarket, frog legs cost more than filet mignon.

Frogs have always played a major role in mythology and fairy tales.

In Jane Yolen's "Tough Magic," the authority on fairy tales points out that the English storyteller has the frog demanding matter-of-factly of the young princess, "Put me in your little bed." And she does, three nights running, before he turns into a prince and marries the girl.

In the German version of the fairy tale, the German princess is not as easily beguiled. She listens to the frog's plea, "Carry me to your bedroom and prepare your silken bed..."

She refuses. But her royal papa orders her to comply. Once in the room, the girl refuses to admit the frog to her bed. Frog threatens to tell Papa, whereupon the princess picks him up and flings him against the wall, shouting "Now you'll get your rest, you nasty frog."

The spattered frog slides down the wall, falls to the floor and turns into a handsome prince.

My favorite frog-prince story involves a frog that jumped out of a ditch and into the path of two spinsters walking along a country road.

"Oh, kind ladies," it croaks, "I am no ordinary frog. Kiss me and I'll turn into a rich Texas oil man."

One of the women reaches down, seizes the ugly, warty creature, thrusts it into her purse and snaps it tightly.

"Why Madge," says her surprised companion. "Aren't you going to kiss the frog?"

"Heavens no!" replies Madge. "Texas oil men ain't what they used to be. I'd rather have a talking frog."

Ms. Yolen notes that the moral behind the frog fairy tales is that "under the warty countenance, under the loathsome skin, there can still beat a princely heart."

When you see a beautiful woman on the arm of an ugly man, don't automatically assume that he was once a frog that didn't quite make it to the magic.

Just believe that beneath his outward appearance there beats a princely heart.

August, 1990

God cranks a lawn mower

After stopping at Omah Boyd's apple orchard, we were winding on slowly through the mountains. Behind me, a man in a pick-up truck was honking his horn.

Oh, the impatient cuss, I thought. Begrudging a city boy his few peaceful hours in paradise.

"He's trying to tell us you left your coat lying on the trunk of the car!" my sister Zetta explained. I wheeled into a side road, got out and retrieved the jacket.

As we resumed our trip, my niece Cecile reprimanded me from the back seat. "Have you thanked the Lord for saving your coat for you?"

"No, I thanked the man in the pickup truck," I said. "The Lord has enough to do without worrying about the coat of an absent-minded tourist on a winding road to Cana, Va."

I should have known better. Pretty soon I was hearing about any number of minor miracles performed for those who have faith the size of a grain of mustard seed.

"God can do all things — great or small," insisted Dot from the backseat.

"Ah, yes," my sister added. "Only last week he started my lawn mower."

"You have to be kidding."

"Not at all. I had worn myself out trying to crank the thing, and when I asked for God's help, it started on the very next try."

Later in the day, I strolled across the highway to visit my sister's neighbor, Phil Dockery. I recounted the tale and asked what he thought.

"I don't want to get involved in that," he chuckled. "But I thought I saw the mailman stop and start that lawn mower for her."

Phil told about the time when he was a boy and a field fire threatened his Aunt Ella's house in the country. She yelled for one of the farm hands who grabbed a broom and started beating out the blaze. With the help of neighbors, the fire was soon out.

"Praise the Lord!" Aunt Ella had said.

And turning to the hired hand, she added, "Sidney, you do know don't you, that the Lord had a hand in this?"

"Yes'm," Sidney agreed. But as he walked away he was heard muttering, "If the Lord had a hand in it he musta set it, 'cause it was mostly me that put it out!"

I went back and confronted my sister. "Phil said it was the mailman who started your lawn mower."

"Oh, that was another time," she said irritably.

"Anyway, who do you think sent the mailman?" asked Cecile, who also thinks God is a mechanic.

"The federal government," I replied. But it was one of those no-win arguments.

I thought of this when I came across an old newspaper clipping that had to do with Sen. Jesse Helms' decision six years ago to run for re-election.

A distraught Jerry Falwell told a Sunday morning audience that the senator had been about to hang up his spurs when he went to him and said, "Senator, you're a national treasure. We can't do without you."

And Jesse is said to have responded, "That's what my grandchildren tell me. I've got my grandchildren growing up and as much as I love my country and my work, I want to watch them grow up."

According to Mr. Falwell, that's when God stepped in and changed the senator's mind.

After hearing this on the air, Jesse confessed to Tom Ellis that it was his wife Dot, not God, who told him to run again.

It happened one night after dinner, after Jesse had dried the dishes. He went in and had it out with her, and she said, "Honey, you've got to run again."

So, here he is again, still neglecting his grandchildren. But he at least has relieved God of the responsibility for his decision.

Meanwhile, we fervently pray that God will abandon all football coaches, women trying to start lawn mowers and "God-chosen" politicians, and concentrate his power on that Mideast madman.

September 1990

Forgiving Pearl Harbor

A news item reports that the Japanese are spending millions trying to improve their public image in America.

Japanese business and industry have increased contributions to good causes in this country from $30 million five years ago to $500 million last year.

It's a noble effort. But one that will take time as well as money. I know more than one person who will never buy a Honda because of what happened Dec. 7, 1941.

Both sides still carry chips on their shoulders.

President Bush plans to visit Pearl Harbor in November. But the White House is refusing Japan's request for a visit to Hiroshima.

"We don't want to give the impression that we were as bad as they were," said an official, explaining why the President won't go.

I doubt that the Japanese who wrote the controversial computer cassette that included the date, December 7, were around when President Franklin D. Roosevelt described December 7 as a day that "will live in infamy."

But when a Florida man whose father was killed in World War II complained, the firm apologized and revised the cassette.

You'd think that something that happened 50 years ago would be history. But it isn't and never will be just history to those Americans who suffered at the hands of the Japanese during World War II and those who, by nature, carry grudges.

It's a two-way street.

Back in 1982, the N.C. Division of Motor Vehicles routinely stamping out new license plates inadvertently printed several hundred plates with JAP on them. Officials and employees of several Japanese firms in the Triangle complained so vociferously that the state promptly recalled the 50 JAP plates it had already sold and trashed the others.

"We felt that to maintain good relations with these people and the Japanese government, we ought to recall the plates," said director Gonzalie Rivers.

I am not as hardnosed as the Confederate army veteran who, on his deathbed, muttered "Fergit, hell!" But I understand where the fellow from Florida is coming from.

One night very long ago, I sat in a communications shack in the New Guinea jungle, listening to Japanese propagandist Tokyo Rose play American hit tunes, interrupting the music with occasional "news flashes" of Japanese military victories.

Suddenly, she interrupted "Don't Sit Under the Apple Tree" with a bulletin: The U.S.S. Franklin, our nation's biggest aircraft carrier, had just been sunk, with all hands lost. My heart skipped a beat. I knew that Arvel, my Marine Corps brother, was aboard the Franklin.

At that moment, I discovered real hate.

Fortunately, Tokyo Rose lied. The badly damaged Franklin, the target of a suicidal kamikaze attack, limped home to later sail again. So did my brother who, for some reason, was the lone survivor of his gun turret crew.

I think my war with the Japanese ended a few weeks after Hiroshima as I sat in a barber shop in the little town of Tachikawa, just outside Tokyo.

As the Japanese barber deftly ran a straight-edge razor over my Adam's apple, I realized what an act of faith it was to climb into that chair.

As the Aug. 14 anniversary of V-J day approaches, it will be easy to stir up old emotions. But if Americans can forgive the Germans for the Holocaust, they should be able forgive the Japanese for the Bataan Death March.

Most of us realize that the Japanese men and women who walk Raleigh's streets today and participate in every aspect of community life had absolutely nothing to do with Japan's sneak attack on Pearl Harbor.

No more than today's young Americans had any part in our government's decision to drop the first atom bomb on Hiroshima.

But forgiving the Japanese for buying Tiffany's is another matter. Fergit, hell!

July 1991

A bit of majesty in us all

From the deck of the ocean-front cottage where we were guests, we could see the steadily bobbing head far out beyond the breakers. I said it looked like a porpoise.

"Oh, no," said one of the women. "It's a man. We saw him yesterday. Several people were on the beach pointing at him, thinking that maybe he had fallen overboard."

Every morning the swimmer plowed his way through the surging sea all the way to the pier. In a while he would be back, the steady strokes of his powerful arms cutting rhythmically along the straight trough in the water.

An incredible feat. For me, walking briskly to the pier and back was a major accomplishment.

"'A full mile!" I'd brag to the others on my return and reward myself with another cup of coffee and breakfast roll.

As we sat on deck, enjoying our mid-morning refreshment, we speculated on the swimmer.

"He has gray hair," said one of our group, focusing the binoculars.

"He's balding in front, probably from years of pushing his head against the waves," said another as the binoculars were passed.

"He's about 55 years old," another added.

"More like 40," I countered.

We made him the owner, not renter, of an ocean-front place. We gave him a wife and two children. We decided he was an athlete in training for a big meet.

Or he could have come to Emerald Isle to recuperate from some great disappointment in life. A death. Or even divorce.

Based only on a distant view of two powerful, churning arms and the occasional glimpse of his head moving up and down in the waves, we wrote the scenario of the swimmer's life. It is a game people play all the time.

"I wonder if he's happy," sighed one of the women.

Ah, happiness — as elusive as quicksilver. So often have I heard my own wife say, "I only want the children to be happy."

Only?

I went inside for a pad and pencil and set out down the beach, walking abreast of the swimmer. I was waiting when, dripping wet, he walked out of the surf.

I said hello to John Johnson of Oak Ridge, Tenn.

A New York native with an engineering degree from Cornell, he was 58, blessed with the body of a man of 35 or 40. What looked like balding through the binoculars was a healthy covering of close-cropped sandy, salt and pepper hair.

A competitive swimmer for 18 years, mastering the long mile non-stop to the pier and back was no big deal to him.

Married? Yes. Father of three, not two, including the son whose graduation from East Carolina University a couple of days earlier had prompted the family's visit to Emerald Isle.

"Are you happy?" I asked. The women back at the cottage would want to know.

"Extremely happy," he chuckled. "And very, very fortunate."

I returned to the cottage just in time to watch the Queen of England being welcomed to America by Congress.

I thought her outfit looked a bit dowdy. The women loved it.

"You can be sure her pearls are real, unlike Barbara's," one of the women noted.

"But I do believe she's a bit one-sided. Notice the way her dress fits at the shoulders," said another.

Ah, Her Majesty, I thought. All that pomp and circumstance. She read her remarks well enough, in her somewhat dreary, dry cereal voice. She's no Churchill, for sure.

She used the Bush words, "naked aggression," a term that always brings to mind the image of soldiers rushing stark naked into battle.

My mind went back to the swimmer and his lonely, mile-long contests with the sea.

The queen is queen by the grace of God and accident of birth. The swimmer has achieved his majesty the hard way. His is the true majesty.

There is a tiny bit of it in all of us.

May 1991

Our Dolly had 'good position'

"I think it's a crying shame that your newspaper has come to the point that a bride has to pay to get her wedding announcement published," an about-to-be bride pouted recently.

"Oh, come now," I teased. "You'll spend more than that on the best man's boutonniere alone. After all, why shouldn't we pay for our vanities?"

There was a time when brides worried more about getting "good position" in the newspaper than anything else about the entire wedding.

The display a bride's photo received in The News & Observer supposedly made a public statement about her social standing.

"Old Raleigh" brides usually got the best play. But if she knew somebody in the "Society Section," even a commoner could hope.

Making it as one of the five or six brides featured on Page One was known as "very good position," as in, "Yes, I was very pleased. Our Dolly got very good position in The N&O."

Page Two was "pretty good position." But if a bride ended up farther back in the section than Page Two, you didn't mention it to members of her family. It was a little like having herpes.

Of course nobody knew until Sunday morning where a bride's photo might appear. Who would be featured on Page One was a closely guarded secret, a decision made solely by the society editor herself.

I was astounded when my wife's wedding photo received "VGP," since she was from out of town and I had been at the newspaper for only a year and had no connections whatsoever with Raleigh's social strata.

But I enjoyed at least a casual friendship with the society editor, who later insisted that our professional association had nothing to do with her decision.

"It was simply because you were finally getting married, A.C. It was Page One news and we played it as Page One news."

Since we were married in Greensboro, I didn't know about our "very good position" until Sunday afternoon, when on the way to Gatlinburg, Tenn. for our honeymoon, we stopped at an Asheville newsstand and bought an N&O.

My wife was pleased until I made the mistake of saying that I thought her figure looked "fuller" in The N&O photo than it had in the Burlington and Greensboro papers.

That remark got the honeymoon off to an icy beginning.

In "Southern Ladies and Gentlemen," Florence King, former staff member of The N&O "Society Section," writes about the trauma of the wedding announcement.

She recalls a distressed mother who came to the newsroom in tears because her daughter's wedding photo "didn't get in!"

"The poor child went down to the hotel lobby at 6 o'clock in the morning to buy this newspaper so she could read her wedding write-up and you didn't put it in!

"Can you imagine what that poor child felt when she realized it wasn't in?" Mama shrieked. "How would you feel, if you didn't get yours in?"

"The members of the Women's Department all agreed that, from a personal standpoint, we could not conceive of a woman who would get out of bed and leave a brand-new husband — or any man — to go and buy a newspaper at 6 o'clock in the morning…" writes Ms. King.

"The reason was perfectly simple. If the wedding write-up did not appear in the paper the very next day, it would mean that they were not officially married. There they were, on their honeymoon, in bed with a man, their virginity gone — and not a word in the paper about it."

The new policy here seems far more democratic because "position" is eliminated. A bride can buy as much space as it takes to satisfy her ego.

And she can be reasonably sure it will get in.

July 1991

Going on 'the pill'

"Why are you having the Lady Baltimore cake?" asked a friend during lunch at Hudson Belk's Capital Room. "I thought you had a cholesterol problem."

"So they say," I added. "But when you take a $1.42 pill every day to take care of the cholesterol, it should also take care of a piece of Lady Baltimore cake once every month."

"Besides," I added, "I just finished reading that Atlantic Magazine article on the cholesterol scare."

Cholesterol readings have replaced replaced golf, sex and acid rain as the number one topic of conversation at cocktail parties. I heard one woman say she is taking an anti-cholesterol drug "that is the rage of Europe!"

Imagine how gratifying it was to learn that I was on the very same pill. It gave me the same warm fuzzy feeling that I imagine folks get from wearing yuppie suspenders and driving a new BMW. I was "in!"

Before I went on the pill, I had tried dieting. But the diet I liked best, my doctor didn't like at all. I will share it with you anyway, so you can grasp its tremendous possibilities and how reluctant I was to give it up.

Breakfast: one-half grapefruit, one slice whole wheat toast, three ounces skim milk.

Lunch: 4 ounces broiled chicken breast, one cup steamed spinach, one cup herb tea, one Oreo cookie.

Mid-afternoon snack: rest of Oreos in box, 2 pints of Rocky Road ice cream, one jar hot fudge sauce, with nuts, cherries, whipped cream.

Dinner: 2 loaves garlic bread with cheese, 1 large sausage, mushroom and cheese pizza, 3 Milky Way candy bars.

A word of advice. Don't run this by your doctor. Chances are he's as unreasonable as mine about this sort of thing.

Like a good businessman, I put my prescription out for bids, checking half a dozen drugstores at least. The high ran to $93 for 60 of the little blue pills, with the low bid coming in at $83.

"Why so much?" I asked a couple of pharmacists. "The stuff's made at Wilson, less than 75 miles away. After all, it's not as if the pills, like those $1 grapefruits in the supermarket, have to be shipped all the way from California."

The pharmacists had no answers. They just seemed happy that the little blue pill was catching on, and was headed for the top of the charts as the "in" pill of the year.

I called the Wilson firm that makes the pill and spoke with the man in charge of answering impertinent questions.

"Now hold on, it's not a pill. It's a tablet," he said, straight off. "Only Carter makes pills."

"OK, OK. But as Gertrude Stein would say, a pill is a pill is a pill — except this one costs $1.42."

The fellow explained that it's the imported chemical that goes into the pill that runs the cost up. At Wilson, they just kind of put the pill together with alcohol, milk, sugar and binders.

As the man said, "It's like making a cake."

Well, according to The Atlantic, 350,000 people were taking the little pill — or tablet — on Dec. 31. That comes to about $500,000 a day. It's probably double that by now. Now that's the kind of cake-baking I'd like to get into.

"Say, do you folks operate an outlet store where perhaps some of us could buy seconds at a more reasonable price?" I asked the pill company spokesman before hanging up.

He laughed, a bit disdainfully. After all, this was not a pantyhose outlet.

Whatever the merits and demerits of this magic pill, I confess it does the job — dropping my cholesterol from 250 to 171 in six weeks. Now I will worry about possible side-effects discussed in the Atlantic article.

Meanwhile, I wish that my mom had patented a medicine that she used to make when I was a kid.

It was called "poplar-bark tea," and it cured everything from homesickness to arthritis. Especially arthritis.

The recipe called for two muscular men to go into the woods and strip the bark from a couple of big poplars. The bark would be cut up in small pieces and placed in a big black pot of boiling water where it would stay for two or three days.

One of my older brothers, a strapping fellow of 30 or so, was bedridden for weeks before he was brought home to be dosed by my mother's magic tea. Once she started ladling tea into him, it took only two days for him to hit the ground running.

I did not learn until years later that the secret "chemical" Mom added to her popular medicine was a dash of "white lightning" which had to be obtained surreptitiously from a certain bootlegger who could be trusted to keep his mouth shut about a highly respected Baptist woman occasionally sending for a bottle of his moonshine.

But it did the job. And she never charged a cent for it. I doubt that the whole pint of moonshine cost $1.42.

I'd like to try poplar bark tea for high cholesterol. But the recipe died with my mother.

September 1989

We are our brother's keeper

A recent U.S. News & World Report article on "The Secret World of Siblings" points out that "sibling relationships — and 80 percent of Americans have at least one — outlast marriages, survive the death of parents, and resurface after quarrels that would sink any friendship."

This doesn't come as news to most of us. That's why we spend our lives trying to patch up frayed relationships that, in most cases, stem from childhood conflicts.

Sibling rivalry is as old as time, beginning with Cain, who slew his brother Abel.

And let's not forget Jacob, who, wearing a goat's hide and pretending to be his hairy older brother, deceived his blind father into giving him Esau's birthright.

A couple of summers ago, my nephew Don and I drove through Wilkes County to the farm where he grew up.

We walked down a path of weeds to the rotting remains of an old tobacco barn that reminded Don of the bitter rivalry between him and his older brother.

"Fred was bigger and could lick me any time," he said, a little sadly. "The only way I could win was with rocks. And he'd go straight to Dad, who would march out to this barn here and make a pencil mark on the wall for each offense.

"After every fifth rock-throwing session, he'd work me over with a hickory switch. But I always made that fifth time count. I chose my rocks carefully. I aimed straight, and I threw hard."

As the youngest in a large family, I was the object of considerable sibling rivalry.

My parents had very little time or attention to lavish on any of us. But to my older brothers, I was the "spoiled one," the Joseph with the coat of many colors, although my coat was of the same plain denim we all wore.

Once, at a family reunion, fed up with being referred to as "spoiled," I confronted my tormentor.

"Tell me exactly. How was I spoiled?" I demanded angrily.

He paused a moment and then said, with a sheepish grin, "Well, during the Depression, Mother let you have grape jelly on your biscuits. The rest of us had to make do with molasses."

I have since apologized for the jelly. But the scars of envy and resentment never heal completely.

The brother nearest me in age was four years older. We co-existed rather well once we reached our teens and were the only children at home. Also, the stark differences in our personalities may have eased the tension.

He was athletic; I was studious. He's a die-hard Republican; I'm a pliable Democrat.

He pulls for Duke; I, for Carolina. When we meet at family reunions, he usually manages some minor put-down, i.e., "You're putting on a little weight" or "Getting a bit gray, aren't you?"

A couple of times, he and I have met for lunch, just the two of us. All the things I planned to say somehow never got said.

I can't help feeling a tinge of guilt over having been born last and eating all that grape jelly. But I'm not so stupid as to think that jelly was the root cause of our estrangement.

The sibling I feared most was a much older brother, the curly-haired, blue-eyed, handsome one. He was coolly aloof, demanding, critical, bordering on cruel.

How I hated the times he "shingled" my hair. It seemed I could never sit still or erect enough to escape his quick anger as he manipulated the clippers and scissors through my hair.

Years later, after he had acquired some measure of respect for me, the awe and fear I had felt toward him gradually changed to admiration and affection. I loved his wit, his self-assurance, his lack of pretension.

At his funeral, I wondered how I could have once disliked so intensely a man that I had come to care for so deeply.

Apparently, such transformation is the exception rather than the rule. Most sibling rivalries endure, from the cradle to the grave.

The magazine article mentioned one fellow, remorse and yearning on his face as he spoke of the older brother "whose friendship was chased away long ago, amid dinner table taunts of 'Porky Pig! Porky Pig! Oink, oink, oink!'"

Because of these deep-seated rivalries, too many siblings deprive themselves of the special closeness, the sharing of memories, and the comfort of knowing that when the going gets tough, a brother or sister will be there to see them through.

We've all seen the familiar photograph of a little boy carrying his brother on his back and the accompanying caption, "He's my brother and he ain't heavy."

It is a touching thought. Unfortunately, that's not always the case in real life.

But not to worry. There's no law that says you have to love your siblings. In fact, the Good Book merely admonishes "Love thy neighbor." Quite frequently, neighbors are easier to love.

February 1994

As useless as peacocks

When I called my sister in the foothills to make arrangements for my upcoming spring visit, she said, "Two of your brothers are here. I'm cooking Sunday lunch for them.

"They're sitting in the living room and having the best time running down Bill Clinton. I just stuck my head in the door and told them I voted for Clinton."

"And what did they say?" I asked.

"They said I ought to be ashamed."

"You ought to tell them you've changed your mind and they can go to the Lantern for lunch," I said.

"Warren wants to speak to you," she said.

"I'm in no mood for losing my temper on Sunday."

"He says he won't mention Clinton."

We had a brief but pleasant conversation. But I'm sure he had to exercise a great deal of willpower.

Being a Democrat isn't easy these days in the foothills, where closet Republicans once kept their politics a closely guarded secret.

My nephew Phil was still smarting from a recent encounter with a friend who had come by to borrow his trailer.

"Dave knows I'm a Democrat," he said. "But that didn't stop him from tearing into Clinton as if he were the Devil himself. Now I like Dave. And I don't mind lending him my trailer at all. But when he brings it back, I plan to find out if he can take it as well as he dishes it out."

Someone once told me that the world's worst losers are N.C. State fans and Republicans. I don't buy that.

I've known plenty of Democrats and Carolina fans who are lousy losers. But after being around my mostly Republican relatives recently, I'm beginning to wonder.

The foothills are fast becoming Limbaugh Land. I wonder if some of these good folks aren't leaving their Bibles at home and heading for church with "I Told You So!" tucked under their arms.

For example, a few Sundays ago, my sister was in the Fairview Church prayer room, where good Christians assemble prior to the regular service to pray for certain individuals, for rain or other pressing needs.

One late arriver said grumpily as he dropped to his knees, "Well, I guess we should pray for that stupid playboy president of ours."

"Are we here to pray for him or crucify him?" my sister had wanted to know.

On Saturday, we drove up to see an elder, ailing brother who lives on Possum Trot Road near the foot of the mountain.

I enjoyed the feeling of isolation as well as the glorious riot of color in my sister-in-law's beds of lilies.

We were sitting in the living room happily chatting about everything in general and nothing in particular when someone knocked at the door.

I let in a fellow who looked the spitting image of Ernest T. Bass, the rock-throwing mountain man in Andy Griffith's Mayberry.

"I was doing some work for the man over on the next farm," he said, without bothering to introduce himself. "I heard this awful racket and I said to the man, 'That sounds like peacocks to me. Anybody 'round here got peacocks?'

"And he said, 'Yeah, Lonnie Snow over on Possum Trot Road, his wife's got peacocks.' And I'm here to tell you I gotta have me some peacocks."

I walked him out to the peacock pen, where he admired the handsome creatures. A male peacock is a sight to behold when it decides to unfold its huge fan of tail feathers.

Writer Flannery O'Connor, who kept peacocks, described the reaction of an old black woman the first time she saw one of the creatures display its splendor.

Stunned by the peacock's spectacular beauty, all she could say was "Amen! Amen!"

When we returned to the house, my sister-in-law told the stranger a female peacock was sitting on a nest of five eggs that should soon hatch. She promised to let him have two chicks at $25 each, which I thought was very reasonable.

I don't know what set the fellow off, perhaps a passing remark or it could be that his politics had ponded up within him and was just ready to overflow. He suddenly stood up and launched into a tirade on the sorry condition of the country and that "sinful man in the White House."

"You must be a Republican," I interrupted.

"I am! How'dja know?" he asked, flashing me an Ernest T. grin.

He finally left, after vowing to return for the peacocks.

John Ruskin once wrote that peacocks and lilies are the most useless things in the world.

I'd add political arguments to his list. At least lilies and peacocks have beauty to recommend them.

May 1994

Pawn shops don't sell myrrh

If you must blame someone, blame the Three Wise Men. After all, it was they who started this business of gift.

In the first place, the Three Wise Men were not only wise but also wealthy. How else could they afford frankincense, gold and myrrh?

When's the last time you checked the shops for frankincense, gold and myrrh?

Oh, yes, frankincense is there in good supply, up to $150 an ounce at the perfume counter where I shop. Gold you can get at your jeweler's, at an astronomical price, of course.

But myrrh?

When I asked a friend where I might find myrrh, he said, "Try the pawn shop. They've got everything else. They must have myrrh."

Dad is the big question mark on many Christmas lists.

I suppose I am as much a problem as columnist Calvin Trillin's Uncle Arthur.

Uncle Arthur, the columnist noted recently, did not play golf or fish and had no hobbies. He already had a radio and earphones. He dressed conservatively and was overstocked with shirts and ties.

Having to choose something for Uncle Arthur was thorn in the flesh of his loved ones.

Uncle Arthur once made a business trip to Kenya. Upon leaving, in order to dispose of the last of the local currency in his pocket, he bought a couple of small made-in-Taiwan elephants at the airport gift shop.

Uncle Arthur is now knee-deep in elephants. He no longer is a question mark at Christmas.

Relatives look down their gift list and sigh happily, "Good old Arthur and his dreadful little elephants." And buy another one.

The same thing happened to me a couple of years ago when just before Christmas I mentioned in my column that I didn't want ties for Christmas, I wanted sunflower seeds.

Both children gave me sunflower seeds. My wife gave me sunflower seeds. Even the guys up at Ace Hardware read the column. I found a 25-pound bag of sunflower seed at my front door on Christmas Eve.

For husbands, choosing the wife's present looms as the most crucial challenge. But I know no man who has to select his wife's gift as if his marriage depended on it.

In Willie Morris' new book, "New York Days," about his tenure as editor of Harper's, he describes the most traumatic Christmas of his life.

On their last Christmas together, his wife made a request, apparently at her analyst's suggestion, that Morris surprise her with a special Christmas gift that would indicate whether or not he was truly attuned to her sensitivities.

Realizing that his marriage and future happiness depended on the gift, Morris spent two or three apprehensive afternoons in Greenwich Village gift shops before finally selecting a beautiful, fragile gold necklace.

On Christmas morning, his wife found it inappropriate.

"That's something you would give to Susie Tucker," she had said, referring to a demurely lovely sorority girl the two had known at the University of Texas.

"Do all defeats, just as victories, come down to one tiny gesture?" Morris asks. "Our marriage ended over a necklace from Greenwich Village, but of course it was more than that."

What was the most memorable Christmas gift you ever received?

My nephew James Sechrist has no trouble remembering his greatest gift.

On a cold Christmas Eve during the Great Depression, James, then 10, worked a street corner hawking the Winston-Salem Sentinel.

James wasn't there to earn money for a bike or pair of skates. As the eldest child in a large family with the father out of work, every cent he earned had to go for food and warmth.

But the newspaper had a policy of giving the newsboys their papers on Christmas Eve. They could keep the whole nickel instead of turning over three cents to the paper.

Also, James' parents had said he could spend this one night's earnings on gifts for his younger brothers and sisters.

As James sat on the curb counting his nickels and dimes and quarters, a bigger boy came along and robbed him of his meager earnings.

He was still sitting on the curb, sobbing his heart out, when the newspaper's editor, having heard of the incident, found him there.

"The stores were open until 12 on Christmas Eve," James remembers. "He took me to Rose's Five and Ten, where he had me name every one of my brothers and sisters.

"He picked out and paid for a gift for each one, and then sent me home in a taxi. It was the first time I ever rode in a taxi.

"Every Christmas since, I think of that night and that man and am reminded that no matter how bad things get, there is somebody out there who cares."

Could this be the myrrh that's so hard to come by? The resin of Christmas?

To all of you, a very "myrrhy" Christmas.

December 1993

Kilroy was always there

You who are under 50 may want to skip today's column. But you are welcome to come along with me on a sentimental journey prompted by the 50th anniversary of "a date which will live in infamy."

Dec. 7, 1941, found me moseying around the house on a Sunday afternoon, doing nothing of consequence. My mother, listening to the Lux Radio Theatre, came to tell me that the program had been interrupted for a dramatic announcement: Japan had bombed Pearl Harbor.

On a warm spring night the following May, as class salutatorian I delivered a corny, emotional speech about our uncertain future. I pledged the class' commitment to preserving "democracy and all that we hold dear."

The Glee Club sang "There'll be bluebirds over the white cliffs of Dover, tomorrow, just you wait and see." The girls cried and the boys bragged about what they were going to do to those "Japs" and "Nazis."

Fifty years later, we relive the fateful day that changed our destiny.

Thanks to the American Legion Auxiliary in Raleigh, I have the Legion magazine's World War II anniversary edition, a rich lode of nostalgia for all who were a part of that time and that war.

Here is a photo of the Betty Grable swimsuit pinup that decorated tents and barracks walls of GIs around the world. And there is a reference to Humphrey Bogart and Ingrid Bergman, who starred in "Casablanca," about lovers torn apart by war.

And there was Kilroy, a mythological character with wide eyes, bald head, long nose and stubby fingers whose face and the caption "Kilroy was here" were scrawled everywhere, on landing barges, latrine walls and captured enemy weapons.

Back home, everybody pitched in, praying, buying bonds, building warships and doing without. In the defense plants, women formed "No work, no woo" clubs and would not date men chronically absent from work.

With gas rationing, an "A" sticker got you three gallons a week. Auto fatalities in New York dropped by 42 percent during the war.

Millions of V-Mail letters crossed the oceans, many marked by a lipstick imprint of a girl's lips and S.W.A.K., sealed with a kiss.

Some, unfortunately, were eventually followed by painful "Dear John" letters that ended with "I hope we can still be friends."

We crisscrossed the country on dirty, sooty troop trains, sleeping sitting up unless we lucked up and drew a Pullman — one man in the upper berth, two sharing the lower.

Before shipping overseas, we were drilled on how to get along with the natives. Soldiers sent to Britain were warned over and over, "Don't steal Tommy's girl."

After four years of war, my mother's four sons all came home. But 292,000 other Americans didn't.

This 50th anniversary may well be the last toast to the last "good war." In Japan, according to a recent New York Times article, the Japanese care even less.

Many blame the United States for the war. Asked about World War II, one Japanese teenager asked, "Who won?"

Fifty years later, we are sometimes tempted to answer, "Japan?"

I leave with you a reminiscence of Thomas E. Woodstrup of Sycamore, Ill., who fearfully rode a minesweeper into Sasebo Bay the day after the Japanese surrendered.

"Had all gotten the word? Were they dug in? Would there be a cross fire?" he wondered, well acquainted with the enemy's treachery.

"We reached the main channel and all guns were manned. The Marines were landing, but there wasn't a soul in sight.

"Then we saw them. The Japanese children waving at us. After four years of hatred, how to respond? No orders covered this. Then a sailor waved back. We had crossed over into peace."

December 1991

Falling out of love raggedly

The couple's table was only a few feet from ours, and we glanced their way more by accident than by intent.

Obviously it was some kind of celebration for them, as it was for us — my wife's birthday.

The waitress went about her work in a businesslike manner, occasionally refilling their glasses with champagne from a silver wine cooler. But there was no toasting, no clicking of glasses.

And no conversation. But these days you often see couples paying more attention to their food than to their soul mates.

The scene prompted my wife to recall an anecdote about a couple in a restaurant.

The woman's lips moved incessantly, while her man sat silent as the sphinx. As they were leaving, another diner approached the woman and complimented her on her animated conversation.

"Oh, I was just repeating the multiplication tables. For appearances' sake," she said. "We ran out of conversation a long time ago."

"They've obviously had a fight," I said of the couple near us.

"Perhaps so," my wife agreed. "He probably was late getting home from work, and when he arrived, the baby sitter had canceled and they had to call his mother. He blew his stack and blamed her."

"And now he's paying for it," I added.

As I observed the couple, I thought of the novel my wife's book club is reading.

"The Ragged Way People Fall Out of Love," by Elizabeth Cox is a sensitive treatment of a marriage coming to an end.

One Sunday afternoon, as the couple sat together with the sound of their children at play coming through the open windows, William said quietly, "I don't love you any more."

"During the year they had been waking at night, both of them, as though an end were coming, as though they expected it to come in the night and surprise them. They didn't yet realize the ragged way people fall out of love."

I would suspect that when conversation dies between a couple, there is something amiss. But you might argue that silence is better than bickering and bitterness.

On the way into the restaurant, we had run into an old friend, along with two other members of the cloth. As we were ordering, the hostess stopped by to say that the gentlemen several tables away had ordered wine for us, in honor of the occasion.

As we acknowledged the gesture with a smile, I couldn't help but contrast the mood of the three priests, laughing and talking together, with the quiet, withdrawn pair only a table away.

Because of their calling, the priests are exempted from the tensions of marital-type relationships.

Yet, also because of their profession, they are privy to the conflicts, the hurts and the raggedness of others falling out of love.

In Ms. Cox's book, when the divorce became final, Molly went to William's office to say goodbye.

"...The sadness for them both was buried in all they had not known. They didn't know how love could end or, if not ended, could collapse upon them. They didn't know how they could fool themselves about what happiness was, and how they thought they could reach it with such ease....Their sadness had more to do with their own amazing ignorance about ways of loving."

Leaving the restaurant, I glanced again at the couple, just in time to see a smile breaking across the woman's face like a single ray of sunlight breaking across a sullen sky.

A welcoming flicker of response creased the man's face.

I know that silence between two people need not be a sickness. On the contrary, it is sometimes a panacea.

And I know that a bystander's imagination can miss the truth by a country mile.

But reciting multiplication tables at dinner is something else. Too often it is just a cover to shut out the sound of "I don't love you anymore."

June 1992

Revisiting old foxholes

Much is being written and said these days about World War II, my war, the last of the "good wars."

But don't go away. I promise not to bore. I had vowed earlier not to inflict a war column on you at all.

That was before I received a card in the mail from Joseph Montuore Sr., who lives at 18 Mapledale Ave. in Succasunna, N.J. The card had to do with bravery.

"I have finally received the Airman's Medal for heroic action in the South Pacific on April 3, 1944," he writes. "I tried for 45 years to be recognized. I wrote to several presidents, congresspersons, politicians, veterans organizations and the Pentagon, with no success.

"I finally located my former commanding officer, Gen. Farmer S. Smith of Raleigh.

"A week later I received authorization for the medal, which he will present to me Sept. 30 at the the 92nd Airborne Squadron's reunion in Savannah, Ga."

What a coincidence. Farmer Smith lives a stone's throw from me. I walked around the block to commend the retired general's deed and learn what a man has to do to win an Airman's Medal.

Joe Montuore's moment in history came on April 3, 1944, on the Nadzab airstrip in New Guinea, when a B-24 bomber failed to become airborne and crashed into another parked plane. Both burst into flames.

Joe, an aircraft mechanic, and four others jumped into a truck, sped to the flaming plane and gathered up five wounded crewmen who had crawled from the inferno.

It was a race against death for all because the bomb load aboard the plane was going to blow at any second.

When it did, shrapnel showered all around the speeding truck as it raced down the runway toward safety.

That's worth an Airman's Medal in my book.

I think most acts of heroism are instinctive. Given time to weigh the odds, most of us would probably stall around until the urge and opportunity to be a hero passes, especially if it might mean being a dead hero.

In Joe's case, my neighbor, the general, assumed that the medal business had been taken care of when he departed for the States, leaving Joe and his buddies behind.

But some armchair officer decided that Joe's heroism wasn't your name-brand heroism, just line-of-duty stuff.

That's usually the way it is when you're not the hero, but only the guy who pushes a pencil in an air-conditioned office.

Anyway, Joe will get his medal, thanks to Farmer Smith, even if it is 45 years late.

I was never called on to be heroic, so I don't know if I could have been or not. I imagine that, like most 18-year-olds, I would have done whatever was required or what I was told to do. Kids obeyed orders back then.

That's what most of us were — just kids. In a recent column, George Will quoted Eugene Sledge, a Marine whose memoir recalls Okinawa, where young replacements died before their units learned their names.

"They were forlorn figures coming up to the meat grinder and going right back out of it like homeless waifs, unknown and faceless to us, like unread books upon a shelf."

As an airman in a troop carrier squadron, I never had to face hand to hand combat and escaped being one of those "unknown waifs" or an unread book, interrupted in mid-chapter by an enemy bullet.

But we buried several of my less lucky friends in lonely graves, now grown over by jungle. We stood at attention as taps sounded and flags were folded, then left them there, lulled in death by gentle waves lapping against long forgotten coral shores.

Some day I would like to do as author William Manchester did in his marvelous book, "Goodbye Darkness."

An ex-Marine who fought the jungle war, Manchester actually retraced his steps, including spending a lonely night in an old foxhole on Guadalcanal.

Memories fade but never quit entirely. A newspaper mention of places like Milne Bay, Nadzab, Dobodura and Okinawa can sweep me back in time to what was and still is a world apart for me.

Or the strains of an old song as I flip the radio dial on the way home from work can do for me what songs did for Manchester, spin the recall button to the time when ships sailed and girls were left behind.

As Manchester says:

"...I think of Taffy whenever I hear the lyrics of those years... there was going to be a certain party at the station, when the lights went on again all over the world; when she wouldn't sit under the apple tree with anyone else but me, and would walk alone, and be so nice to come home to, till the end of time. Thanks for the memory, Taffy. Here's looking at you, kid."

For all who have been to war, or shared a war, these flashbacks sneak in and out of our lives, 'til the end of time. Our time.

September 1989

Executioners can be gentle, too

Not long ago, during the "recent unpleasantness" at N.C. State, I was introduced to someone who, during a pause in conversation, asked what I did for a living.

When I answered, there was a cold, "Oh," and another long pause in conversation. Why is it that what we do tends to stereotype us as to who we are?

Imagine, if you will, the scenario in which the answer to the "What do you do?" question might go something like this, "Oh me? I'm the guy who throws the switch at Central Prison's executions."

We might immediately assume that anyone with such a job is a total washout, something less than a human being. We could be wrong.

I once interviewed such a person. His job was pulling the switch that dropped the deadly little gas pellets under the chair at the Central Prison gas chamber.

While he was not a life-of-the-party type, he had a family and kids, went to church, undoubtedly loved and was loved. He said he slept well at night and, like most of us, thought he was grossly underpaid for the work he did.

A man's job does not make the man. I read somewhere that even Anne Boleyn's executioner was not without compassion.

He was so impressed by her spunk — she refused to be blindfolded — that, as Anne knelt at the block, he persuaded a spectator to divert her attention so he could slip up on her and administer the coup de grace.

Ah, stereotypes. Farmers are among the few people still perceived as good guys in our society. Ask one at the Farmer's Market if his Silver Queen corn was picked fresh this morning rather than in yesterday's heat. He will look you in the eye, and say, "Yes, sir! Can't you see my britches' legs are still wet with morning dew?" And we believe him.

Yet, an equally honest used car salesman traditionally places near the bottom on the public trust charts, only slightly ahead of newspapermen.

Recently, in Surry County, after a young Baptist minister delivered a very moving sermon, I waited around to compliment him.

"I used to be a car salesman," he said, by way of explaining his persuasive talent. "A new car salesman," he hastened to add.

Ministers are especially vulnerable to stereotyping. We tend to strip preachers of their human traits and frailties and expect them to live like practicing saints.

Dr. William Simpson Jr., the new pastor at Edenton Street Methodist

Church, was getting a haircut recently when the barber asked the inevitable question, "What do you do for a living?"

"I sell fire insurance," the minister replied. It was not an outright falsehood.

"Being a preacher, in a way I do," Dr. Simpson chuckled. He knew that if he answered "I'm a preacher," the whole tone of the barber shop conversation would change abruptly.

Years ago, when he was pastor of a Kitty Hawk church and making the long trip to Raleigh for occasional church meetings, Dr. Simpson would stop for gas at a certain country store along the way.

A small crowd of loafers, mostly rural folks in bibbed overalls, would be sitting around the store.

But one morning he noticed among the overalled clientele a newcomer wearing a business suit and drinking from a bottle that clearly was not a "big orange drank," as Andy Griffith would say. It was obvious that man had been there for awhile.

As the minister paid for the gas, the store owner spoke his usual "Thank you, preacher." The man in the blue suit strolled over.

"You really a preacher?"

"Yes, I am."

"Well, I guess you think I got no business doing what I'm doing."

"It doesn't matter what I think," the minister said.

"Well, I just come down here from Raleigh once in a while to get away from it all and let my hair down," the man explained.

A pretty girl back home was dating a young man who had a summer job at the chicken-processing plant.

"I don't know how she stands dating somebody who spends all day cutting off the heads of chickens," a relative worried.

What the boy did by day shouldn't make him a less exciting date at night. Years ago, a rough, tough ex-Marine worked in The Raleigh Times sports department. At least we thought he was tough.

But before every date with the dentist, he would drive his cohorts up the wall with his constant whining and complaining about the dreaded rendezvous.

Finally, one said, "Bob, you're nuts. Here you are carrying on like a 6-year-old about going to the dentist when you have served in the Marines, played tackle for the Baltimore Colts and been shot twice in Korea."

"I know, I know," sighed the big fellow. "But I was never shot in the teeth!"

What we do usually reflects our interests. But it doesn't totally define us as individuals. As the poet said, "We are what we are."

October 1989

One sour note, you're out!

You may or may not remember a column I wrote some time ago. It was dubbed "The First Violinist."

In it, I compared the accomplishments of a favorite Latin teacher to the first violinist in a symphony.

In the column, I made the mistake of saying that the violinists are always there sawing away, while the percussionists can take a stroll downtown for a beer or read "War and Peace" between the infrequent moments when they must perform.

I also made the mistake of assuming that everyone, including percussionists, has a sense of humor. Too often what is spoken in jest is taken seriously. It's not surprising that I have had my ears pinned back — deservedly — by a percussionist in the North Carolina Symphony.

In addition to stressing my ignorance of music, a charge to which I plead nolo contendere, she taught me something — about both music and human nature.

She pointed out, among other things, that while the violinists and their string-playing compatriots each, for the most part, studied one instrument, the percussionist has to study all the standard orchestral percussion instruments, often as many as 10.

"The violinists, 'sawing away through the whole piece' may miss a note or two and few will notice (there's safety in numbers, Mr. Snow)," she said.

"But a percussionist's job can be on the line for that one triangle note or cymbal crash, and percussionists have indeed been known to lose their jobs over just one note.

"The great composers dole out percussion sounds very carefully in their writing because, among other reasons, they know that like precious gems, those sounds are not suited to every musical occasion.

"Likewise, the musicians who produce those sounds in a truly musical way are worth their weight in gold."

I have long realized and respected the pressure on the solo performer, no matter what the circumstances.

For example, imagine the sheer anxiety the receiver feels on the opening kickoff as, alone downfield, he awaits the descending pigskin.

With 60,000 pairs of eyes on him, he is surely praying, "Oh, God! Please don't let me drop it!"

Then there is that fear of forgetting your lines in the school play. Leaving your Rotary Club speech at home on the kitchen table. Or freezing up during a public performance.

My wife often relives the nightmare in which she, at age 12, sat down to play "The King Cotton March," in a piano recital.

Confidently, she glided through the first two measures. Then suddenly, nothing more would come. After her third false start, the teacher stalked on stage and placed the music before her. Only a remarkable youngster can survive such an experience without scars.

There is certainly enough pressure in the newspaper business. It isn't easy to crank out copy with an impatient editor hanging over your shoulder and the second hand on the big clock sweeping toward the one o'clock deadline.

I remember one reporter who broke under such pressure.

"Dammit!" he screamed hysterically. "Get away from me! Get away from me!" We scattered for the moment. But everyone in the newsroom knew he was in the wrong business.

Yes, many of us work under deadline. Farmers race against rain at hay harvest. Businessmen must come up with budgets.

But these perform in the relative seclusion of the newsroom, the field or the corporate office. "Violinists," they can play off-key and few notice.

Not the percussionists. They are out there at center stage or on the 5-yard line, alone in the spotlight, with the whole world watching. I salute them.

September 1991

President Clinton's $4 skivvies

Knowing that President Clinton gives his worn-out underwear to charity makes him quite human.

But charging off a $4 tax deduction for every pair donated while he was governor of Arkansas may not be politically correct.

I rarely if ever donate used skivvies to charity. If I did, I certainly wouldn't claim tax credit for them as I would, say, for a coat with six-inch lapels or a pair of cuffless pants.

On the other hand, doting Democrats can reasonably argue that Clinton's well-traveled underwear would bring a small fortune at public auction.

They might say that the underwear's value may have increased by the mounting reports, few if any proved, of his incredibly lusty rounds of womanizing during his Arkansas years.

A local Salvation Army employee I talked to yesterday said, yes, donors do sometimes donate skivvies that have seen better days and can't be recycled. But they also receive some in good condition, and frequently even brand-new underwear.

"We sure can use men's underwear," she added. "We never seem to have enough."

On the way to lunch I stopped at Hudson Belk's underwear counter and learned that a pair of men's undershorts can cost up to $25 for the brightly flowered designer types.

Tell me. Who are these crotch-conscious peacocks who indulge in such silky extravagance anyway?

When I was a kid, underwear was never a big deal. We wore long-handles from late September until May 1, when we were allowed to shed the things, no matter if the temperature stood at 20 or 80 degrees on April 30. Not a day earlier, not a day later.

From then until frost, we went sans underwear, except on Sundays to church.

When you have to do laundry by hand, you do everything possible to reduce the wash load.

During lunch, someone brought up the matter of President Clinton's tax deduction.

"You don't understand," said Dave. "The fair value of such a donation depends on who has been inside the underwear. A pair of George Washington's underwear would be worth a fortune right now. Wouldn't you like to own a pair of Elvis Presley's old skivvies?"

"The very idea turns my stomach."

"Well, what about one of Dolly Parton's discarded bras?"

"Now that's a different matter," I laughed.

Parting with clothes is easier than disposing of life's other mementoes. My wife lets go with even greater reluctance.

Cleaning out my storage house recently, I came across the door to the children's long-gone treehouse. It is all that's left of the childhood castle once wedged between two maple trees on the back lawn.

Time and time again, I have put out the door with its Plexiglas window for the trashman, only to find it has mysteriously reappeared.

But I'm also guilty. I can't let go of my old Air Force uniform. Or the journal I kept during my sojourn through the South Pacific. The amateurish writings of a scared, homesick 18-year-old have been heaved trashward more than once, only to be reclaimed — by me.

Each time I clean out closets, a sad song runs through my mind: "There's nothing left for me, of things that used to be. I live in memory, among my souvenirs."

Disposing of a wartime diary is small potatoes compared to the dilemma facing Samuel Marks of Chapel Hill, whose collection of combat souvenirs includes items from Adolph Hitler's bunker.

A member of the 82nd Airborne Division, Sam was among the first occupation troops in Berlin. Russian occupation authorities rewarded a few Yanks for their help in winning the war by taking them to the bunker where Hitler and mistress Eva Braun lived and died.

"Windows were broken, walls were cracked, furniture removed or destroyed, and everywhere rubble," Sam writes. "We were left alone to wander about. Knowing that my wife was maintaining an album of wartime memorabilia at home, I was determined to send her some items from this historic hell."

From the Hall of Mosaics, Sam took pieces of brightly colored stones. He picked up an aqua wall tile from Hitler's bathroom, chips from the Fuhrer's smashed desk, and finally, a small piece of colorful fabric from a broken chair.

Back at his unit, Sam mounted the souvenirs on file cards, labeling them: "Spoiled Splinters from Hitler's Table Top," "Fabric Filched from a Fauteuil," "Personally Picked Pieces from the Hall of Mosaics." The bathroom tile he labeled, "Tile Taken from a Tyrant's Toilet."

Those are souvenirs worth saving. But my war diary, too tame for a TV movie, is practically worthless, unless I can consign it to the paper recycling basket and claim a tax deduction.

It might be worth half a pair of well-worn presidential skivvies. But I doubt it.

December 1993

A best seller with spaghetti

He called me to ask me to go to lunch and read the first chapter of a possible novel. He sounded so excited, so enthusiastic, how could I refuse?

Enthusiasm in anyone is becoming a rare phenomenon.

The idea of the book had hit him as he was driving alone to the beach. He had passed a church with one of those curbside neon signs announcing next Sunday's sermon.

"There was my title!" he said, his face alive with excitement. "Hell Has No Fire Escape."

"A novel is quite an undertaking," I said. "I've never had the nerve to tackle one. You have to have a vivid imagination, for one thing."

"Imagination? Man, I plan to build it around my own life experiences. It's gonna be autobiographical."

And he gave me some examples.

Obviously, the young man has lived a lot, beginning as early as 18 when he was a lifeguard at the beach.

One day a middle-aged woman came up to him and said, "How would you like sex in a different way?"

"How different?" the young man asked cockily, confident that he had little left to learn in that department.

"How about in a bathtub filled with spaghetti," the woman had said and passed on down the beach.

I know several people who are obsessed with the idea of writing a novel. "Acute Novelitis" usually hits sometime between 30 and 40, when life is complicated by young children, a home mortgage and a 10- to 20-year marriage.

Instead of having an affair, buying a Porsche or just going out for a pack of cigarettes and never coming back, these men dream of writing a novel.

My young friend is a promising writer. And as he said, he's read some lousy stuff that has made the New York Times best seller list. So have I.

He's also on the right track by wanting to base his book on actual experience. Thomas Wolfe insists that all good writing has its root in personal experiences. If I ever wrote a novel, mine would have to be based on fact.

Just how much of yourself do you give to a novel, or even to a column? Each author must decide for himself.

One of my favorite writers, Nelson Algren, once had an affair with a woman who wrote about their relationship in a novel, quoting extensively from his love letters to her.

The concerned publisher called Mr. Algren to get his OK.

He said he thought about it for a few days before giving his reluctant approval, only to have second thoughts later.

"Hell," he said, "love letters should be private. I've been in whorehouses all over the world and the women there always close the door, whether it's in Korea or India.

"But this woman flung the door open and called in the public and the press. Other women then began to write me and even came knocking at my door. God, it was terrible."

I was disappointed that my friend was not writing his novel simply because his soul cried out to be heard and read. He was very up front about it.

"I need the money," he said. "And I would hope that there might be revenue from the movie."

Then he started wondering who might be the best actor to play himself in the film version.

I cautioned him about the title he had copied from the Baptist church marquee.

"You have to be careful. Some folks might think it's a religious tract," I warned. "You don't need that if you're hoping for a best seller."

With that in mind, I wished my friend good luck with his novel. I shall monitor its progress with interest. But in parting I advised him to think twice about including the incident of the spaghetti in a bathtub.

Since he is married, he can't afford to have strange women knocking on his door.

September 1990

Spend it all for loveliness

Here it is, the day after Christmas, and I want to share with you a few of my favorite things, items that didn't come in my Christmas stocking.

Just before Christmas, the Fourth Wise Man made an appearance at the North Hills K&W Cafeteria, where my wife had taken my mother-in-law to lunch. He was wearing the uniform of the Raleigh Police Department.

As they were preparing to leave, the elderly woman studied the man at the next table and read his shoulder patch.

"Hmm. Capital City Police," she mused. "My good man, it's a comfort to know we were being watched over by the Capital City Police. It's especially comforting to my daughter, who worries about me incessantly. Tell me, sir, when do children stop worrying about their parents?"

The officer smiled and looked her in the eye: "Ma'am, they stop worrying when they stop caring."

Speechless, this good woman who usually knows all the answers turned and walked away without a word.

My pre-Christmas stocking included a wonderful belly laugh, compliments of Suzanne Britt, who told me about a New Yorker cartoon she stores in her memory and trots out every Christmas when she hears "Joy to the World."

The cartoon depicts a dreary apartment where a bedraggled looking wife, her hair in curlers, is at the sink addressing a high stack of dirty dishes, pots and pans.

The woman's husband, wearing a hard hat and clutching his lunch pail, is coming in the door.

He says "Hi, honey. I'm home!"

And she says, "Let heaven and nature sing!"

From my faithful Apex correspondent, who knows my addiction to bumper stickers on other people's cars, I received a heart-warming one for my holiday enjoyment.

As she was driving through Rosaryville, Md., on her way home from a pre-Christmas trip to Philadelphia, she was passed by a car driven by a man of the cloth.

His bumper sticker read "My Boss is a Jewish Carpenter."

A Christmas memory I treasure was the first Christmas card of the season. It came from a Wake Forest reader who said simply, "Christmas is a new column by A.C. Snow."

Columnists are hopelessly as addicted to flattery as the next person.

After all, readers are their reason for being.

I opened the card on the way to coffee with my friend Scrooge. When I shared it with him, I didn't even mind his saying, "Oh my, some poor soul is hitting the eggnog early."

A week or so before Christmas, I journeyed back to the foothills and spent 45 minutes strolling through my quiet, peaceful two-stoplight hometown.

I stopped in at a bank to cash a check made out to me.

"Now you don't know me, and I'm from Raleigh, but I wonder if you could cash this," I began, prepared to drop a few prominent local names such as Snow, Cooper and Folger.

I didn't need to. The young woman was already counting out the bills. No identification demanded.

At the post office, where I bought stamps, a friendly woman took time out to talk to me about commemorative stamps.

"Elvis will be in on Jan. 8," she said. "We've ordered 30,000!"

O Little Town of Anywhere.

And, on a rainy day, at the Tavern on the Green Restaurant in New York, my friend Mary Lib Finlator, between the main course and dessert, served up a side order of Sara Teasdale that should guide us through the year:

Spend all you have for loveliness
Buy it, and never count the cost;
Buy one white singing hour of peace
Count many a year of strife well lost.

December 1992

'Don't tell God I'm drunk!'

At a pre-Christmas party, a woman came up to me and said, "I have had two face-to-face conversations with God."

This is not the sort of thing you ordinarily hear at parties. Caught off guard, I blurted, "What did you two talk about?"

She said it happened after she was critically injured in an automobile accident. She had actually gone through the tunnel of death and come face-to-face with God.

"And I said 'God, I didn't even get to say goodbye to the children.'"

"And He said, 'Your children need you more than they need their father,' and he sent me back to life."

The incident came to mind as I read Newsweek magazine's recent cover story, "Talking to God," which noted, among other things, that though only 40 percent of Americans go to church, 85 percent talk to God.

Newsweek says more people will pray this week than go to work, exercise or have sexual relations.

Few of us have the face-to-face conversations with God my friend talked about. And, somehow, talking to the Almighty seems to come more simply and naturally at the seashore or in the mountains. God's majesty seems more overpowering there than it does in Crabtree Valley traffic.

In my sister's foothills church, they pray a lot.

One Sunday, the church bulletin included the caption, "Pray for the Sick," followed by several names. Then came "Pray for the Lost," followed by six other names, including the name of Pearl White, a fine Christian woman who ran the country store we patronized when I was a kid.

"Is Pearl lost?" I asked my sister after church.

"Of course not!" she snapped. "Why?"

When I pointed to the 'Pray for the Lost' and the names under it, she said, "Oh, that has nothing to do with Pearl. That means pray for the lost, whoever they are. Pearl's just been sick."

Every Sunday night of my childhood, my father called his family together for prayer. We would kneel by our chairs while Dad carried on what seemed an interminable conversation with God.

He left nothing to chance, especially where the crops were concerned. In summer, he prayed for rain; in autumn, for good prices on the tobacco market. I remember still, with envy, the childlike faith and sincerity with which he prayed.

Some people pray consistently. Others only when they're in trouble, much like the fellow who, on an extended drunk and fearing that he was dying, asked his wife to pray for him.

When she began with "Oh, Lord, have mercy on my poor drunk husband," the miserable man pleaded, "Shhhh! Don't tell the Lord I'm drunk! Tell Him I'm sick!"

We often pray selfishly. I once overheard a woman telling another that while rushing to the hairdresser's she had asked God to turn all the traffic lights green.

"He did. Otherwise I would never have made it!" she said confidently.

I don't agree with those who insist that nothing is off-limits in prayer. For example, I don't believe God wills one sports team to win over another.

Last year, after the Chicago Bulls won the world championship, the first thing the team did was thank God for the glory of the moment.

"It was only with God's blessing that we were able to do it," said Craig Hodges. "I'm humbled just to know that God accepted us, that He felt we were worthy of this day."

At least the team had the good grace to give thanks. Too often we are so busy saying "Gimme, God," we forget to say "Thanks, Lord."

It's not surprising that in these uncertain times 85 percent of us pray. Someone once said, "There are no atheists in foxholes."

There are very few in today's economic foxholes.

January 1992

A common man's kind of car

It's time to trade cars. I dread the looking, the negotiating and the final decision. And saying goodbye to the 1984 Chevrolet Celebrity that has become such a steadfast, reliable friend for 72,000 miles isn't easy.

My friend Glenn Keever thinks I should see a psychiatrist.

"Buying a new car should be as exciting as casting about for a new wife — if you were in the market," he said. "And it has none of the risks."

He has a way with cars, while my relationship extends primarily to getting in, turning on the switch and letting four wheels take me where I want to go.

"No matter what you say, the car a man drives makes a statement," my friend insisted. "A man in your position must rise above a Celebrity."

"But I like this car better than any I've ever owned," I argued. "Better even than that 1957 Carolina-blue Ford convertible with the steel top that folded itself and disappeared into the trunk."

"Now that was a statement car," he said. "Remember, you were a bachelor then. You were out trawling for girls with that car. And it paid off handsomely. You got your wife.

"First, consider the fact that you have daughters who sooner or later are going to get married," he continued.

"Do you want to drive up to the church in a 1984 Celebrity with plain hubcaps?

"And when they ask 'Who giveth this woman' and you say 'Her mother and I', do you want everybody in the church thinking, 'He's still driving that 1984 Celebrity with standard hubcaps and 72,000 miles — mostly city?'"

Last year, I lost — or someone stole — the hubcap from the right-hand front wheel. Its absence did not greatly bother me, but it almost gave my friend an ulcer.

Finally, I drove out to Hubcap Annie's, had a delightful visit with her and came away with a $30 hubcap.

"I hope you're happy. I replaced the hubcap," I said next day to my friend.

Instead of congratulating me, he said, "It's the only clean thing on the whole car. When are you going to wash and wax that vehicle?"

As we walked out of The Cafe, where we were having coffee, he pointed to a car parked at the curb.

"Now that's what you need. A Mercedes. Maybe $60,000 or so."

"Ye gods!" I exclaimed. "It has windshield wipers on the headlights! How gauche."

"Think of your image," he said calmly. "If not for yourself, then for your wife and children."

"Undoubtedly the headlights turn themselves off automatically," I said, remembering one night several years ago in the Reynolds Coliseum parking lot where a woman walked away from her car with the lights still on.

"Ma'am, you've left your lights on," I said, like the Good Samaritan that I am.

"They turn themselves off," the woman said haughtily, her nose in the air.

"Hell will freeze over before I remind anybody else to turn off her headlights," I said to my wife. "I'm tempted to let the air out of her tires to see if they pump themselves up automatically."

"I understand that the Mercedes is the ultimate car," I mused.

"Yes, but you can't afford it," my friend said. "And even if you could, you wouldn't want to buy a bottom-of-the-line Mercedes. When it comes to making a statement, that would be like buying a secondhand Cadillac."

I have top-of-the-line tastes in some things. It's just that a car is not one of them. I am tempted to just keep the old Celebrity, have it waxed and fix the small dent that a runaway Harris-Teeter grocery cart recently put in the door.

Oh, I know I'll trade cars. But the only statement I want my new car to make is that it belongs to a common man and is probably paid for.

October 1990

Don't forget when they hugged

I was standing in line for a cup of coffee at a fast-food restaurant when a toddler who had wandered away from her mother rushed up and hugged my leg tightly.

I looked down into an innocent little face dominated by a toothy smile and large, glowing brown eyes.

"Aha, they have missed one," I thought. "There is one child left who has not been told to beware of strangers, one who has not been ordered not go near a man because the man will do bad things to her."

For those whose children have outgrown their once spontaneous rapture at beholding their parents, being hugged by a child is special.

Teens should sport bumper stickers: "Have you hugged your Dad today?"

There are two sides to these brief excursions into nostalgia land.

During a beach trip with some friends, we ate at a rustic seafood restaurant. At the adjoining table were two young couples and four small children, all of whom appeared to be under 4.

The youngest, a doll-like girl in a high chair, clamored for attention, banging a rattle on her plate and shrieking loudly every few seconds.

The father, deeply involved in conversation with the other man at the table, momentarily forgot the baby, who toppled head-first from the high chair.

There was a moment of terrifying silence as we all stared at the baby on the floor. The mother's face turned ashen.

Finally, the child burst into piercing screams, announcing she had not been killed on impact. A good sign. A welcome sign.

"There goes the weekend for that poor guy," sympathized one of my group. "See. His wife is already giving him hell for letting the kid fall on its head."

One of the little boys had to go to the bathroom. His father took him. The other little boy, noting his buddy's absence, asked, "Where's Jimmy?"

"Jimmy's gone to the bathroom."

"I wanna go to the bathroom, too!" he yelled.

So went the evening. The baby was put on the floor to play with Mom's handbag, which she quickly emptied on the rough boards.

She crawled under an adjoining table occupied by three roughly dressed fishermen. The baby pounded on one diner's foot with the hairbrush from her mother's purse.

The parents eventually missed the baby. There was momentary panic until the mother rescued her from beneath the strangers' table, apologizing to the fishermen.

"I wish my wife could share this," I said. "She is always sighing about how wonderful it was when the kids were little and so much fun."

"Yeah, me, too," said one of my friends. "With four kids under 10, eating out was always a nightmare for us.

"As soon as my tribe marched into a restaurant, all the waitresses would mysteriously disappear. Or when forced to, would approach our table with the enthusiasm of a brave soldier facing a firing squad.

"Ordering always provoked a fight. I would say 'Bring two of the 8-ounce rib-eyes and four hamburgers with French fries.'

"'Let them order for themselves,' my wife would say. 'They are mature individuals!' Actually they were spoiled kids.

"So we'd end up with six steaks, four barely touched, and a bill that kept us on bread and water until next payday."

When my children were toddlers who loved to be cuddled, who adored us and were dependent on us, we wished they were older, so we could have more freedom and less work.

And when the children got older, and more independent than we wanted them to be, and didn't want to be cuddled, we wished they were the way they were when we wished they weren't the way they were.

But I still miss, now and then, the feel of small arms around my neck and the worshipful whisper of "Daddy!" in my ear.

January 1990

Bored stiff in Billings, Montana

The small rhubarb started when, working at my computer in the sports department, I heard Tim Stevens at the next "work station" (it used to be a desk) say, "Yeah, Billings, Montana is a wonderful place to be if you like to sleep."

I learned later that he was commiserating with Garner's young Patrick Watkins, who is playing with a minor-league baseball team in that far away town.

Ann Berry, who had dropped by to take me to coffee in the snack bar, overheard the comment about Billings.

She bristled, as she characteristically does on behalf of the abused, the downtrodden and lost causes in general.

"How can you say such a thing?" she asked when Tim got off the phone. "Around Billings you have some of the best trout fishing in the world. Yellowstone National Park is only four hours away. Around Billings, you can hunt anything up to and including elk, moose, bear and girls.

"It's gorgeous, wild country. And Ted Turner and Jane Fonda's ranch is a mile away."

No, Ann isn't from Montana. She grew up with Dorothy in Oz country. But she once lived at Bozeman, a boulder's throw from Billings.

"Now all that may be fine and good if you're a tourist," Tim retorted. "But it doesn't mean much to a young guy who has to be at the ballpark at 2 p.m., stays there until 1 a.m. and falls in bed at 3 a.m.

"Sure, he has his mornings free. But not many bears or girls are moving around during those hours."

I cite this little anecdote to illustrate how sensitive we are to criticism of places in the heart — especially the home places.

Not long ago, reporter Rob Christensen wrote a piece about North Carolina being the front-runner among 92 cities and 17 states to land a $300 million Mercedes-Benz assembly plant.

Rob cited a sorry, low-down piece by Philadelphia Inquirer columnist David Johnston in which Johnston shows exceedingly poor taste and ignorance by putting down a state he knows next to nothing about.

Johnston asks if the Germans want to send their "educated, cultural and politically sophisticated executives to a comparative cultural Sahara."

"Will its best and brightest want to raise their children in a place where the government subsidizes farmers to grow cancer sticks and the senior senator may mistake 'Gotterdammerung' for a swear word?"

Obviously, Mr. Johnston hasn't ventured beyond his city's limits in some time.

Our man Christensen goes on to cite the many sophistications of our beautiful and exciting state, including our first-class state symphony directed by Gerhardt Zimmermann, a guy who for years has toted water to this cultural desert. Columnist Johnston's message from the City of Brotherly Love truly has a Cain and Abel touch.

I have little patience with those who take swipes at cities or states or regions for no good reason whatsoever.

Another case in point is columnist Dave Barry's latest book, a paperback posing as a travel guide.

It is solely a commercial venture, a literary rip-off, a trivial two-day production from an otherwise talented writer.

Right off, he cheats North Carolina by lumping it in the same paragraph with North Dakota, simply because they're both "Norths."

Our state is wrapped up in two sentences: "The major products of North Carolina are tobacco and enormous amounts of phlegm. North Carolina also contains the famous 'Lost Colony;' ask anyone for directions."

Talk about phlegm!

When I called the Billings (Mont.) Gazette to ask "What do you do on a rainy night in Billings?" the 2 p.m. temperature there was 74 degrees. It was 96 in Raleigh.

My question released a veritable deluge of statistics and serendipities from Chris Myers, editor of the paper's Enjoy section.

"Billings is the liveliest town in the Rockies," she said. "Two hundred nights of musicians and poets, good restaurants, two colleges, a center for writers…"

"But what does an 18-year-old baseball player do for fun?" I interrupted.

"There you go, stereotyping a baseball player as being totally out of tune with culture," she chastised.

We agreed that Patrick, considering his profession, would probably do about the same thing he would do if he were playing in Raleigh. Except that here he has his friends and family. In Billings, he is a stranger, far from home.

Actually, I don't think chasing bears and girls in Billings, Montana, would be bad, as long as you were careful not to catch the bear.

Still, I would hope that somebody in Billings might invite young Patrick to lunch on his day off. At least once.

July 1993

Much ado over aviation and sex

I was unloading the car for a few days at Windward Dunes at Indian Beach when manager Kevin Willis strolled up.

"Say, how come you're writing about sex so much lately?"

"What are you talking about?" I flared.

"Now don't get mad at me," he said defensively. "I just overheard two guys out by the newspaper rack say this morning, 'Wonder why A.C. Snow's writing about sex so much.'"

I racked my brain. I hadn't written anything about sex, except to mention a cat trying to get pregnant under my bedroom window. They must have me mixed up with Ann Landers or Lewis Grizzard.

Or Madonna, who has just written a book titled "Sex," which the publishers hope to sell for $50 a whack.

Anyway, why don't these people pick on TV? Even "The Golden Girls" are talking dirty.

And what about bookstores? They have whole sections on sex — mainly "how to" books that tell folks how to do what nature itself teaches them to do.

Someone recently directed my attention to a 1938 book written by E. B. White and James Thurber called "Is Sex Necessary?"

In this wonderful spoof on the sexologists of that day, the authors conclude, "Two factors in our civilization have been overemphasized. One is aviation, the other is sex. Neither is entitled to the space it has been accorded. Each has been deliberately promoted."

The authors noted that few people are fitted for flying, whereas everyone is fitted for sex.

Because there seemed to be a general lack of interest in sex, the challenge was to make sex seem more complex and dangerous than it was. So, sexologists to the rescue! Soon the country became flooded with books on sex.

"To prepare for marriage, young girls no longer assembled a hope chest — they read books on abnormal psychology," wrote White and Thurber. "If they finally did marry, they found themselves with large numbers of sex books on hand but almost no pretty underwear."

The authors pointed out that, since the Garden of Eden, men have been the aggressors, with women being more reticent.

Out of the female's reticence came the art of fudge-making as a device to fend off the aggressive male.

"The flitting from table to stove, the constant necessity of stirring the boiling confection, the running out of doors to see if the candy had cooled and hardened served to abort any objective demonstrations at all on the part of the male," the authors said.

Soon, the rejected males began to draw apart, producing the psychic condition "which caused the adult to remain in a state of suspended love, as if he were holding a bowl of goldfish and had nowhere to put it."

Out of this frustration, the den was invented, "full of paperweights and other bric-a-brac," into which the male retreated.

And, as we all know, he is there today, a couch potato watching Monday night football.

Today, there is precious little left of the mystery of sex that enveloped my childhood.

My mother once told me that she never kissed my father until after they were married. Nice girls didn't.

At home, the word "sex" never existed, although our large family was certain evidence that sex was practiced with great enthusiasm.

I was not alone. A cloud of ignorance hovered over most of us until high school, although puberty raged through our gangly bodies well before then.

My first view of the female form sans clothes came when I opened a trunk containing my older sister's nursing school textbooks. Discovered in the act of drinking deeply from this newfound fount of knowledge, I was severely punished for my curiosity.

Yet somehow we learned all we needed to know without the benefit of whole shelves of explicit instruction at the bookstores.

"See! He's at it again — another column on sex," my critic is saying. Wrong! This is a column about the overemphasis on sex.

September 1992

Leave love letters in sand

One of my daughters not long ago asked her mother if she had kept the letters I wrote her during our courtship, while she was working on a graduate degree at Northwestern University and I was plugging away as city hall reporter for The Raleigh Times.

"Yes, they're in the attic," she said. "But they're not the kind of letters that are likely to set off spontaneous combustion and burn down the house."

I couldn't argue with her. The men in our family have tended to be a cautious lot, not excessively demonstrative and not prone to penning paeans of passion. But only one of 10 brides abandoned ship before reaching port.

I don't know if young people write love letters anymore. It is my opinion most don't write letters of any kind, depending rather on the telephone as their medium of expressing affection from afar. It's just as well.

Not long ago, I was allowed to share a box of old love letters written by a college student to the woman he later married — and divorced.

The outpouring of tenderness and affection in the boy's letters later were betrayed by time and temptation.

Prowling through my files, I unearthed a clipping about the death of Margaret Polk, whose pretty likeness was painted on the nose of the famous "Memphis Belle," the first B-17 to survive 25 World War II missions over enemy territory.

It was the custom then for combat crews to name planes for girlfriends, hometowns and movie stars. A soldier with a flair for art could pick up extra bucks by decorating the bombers and transport planes with slogans or sexy female figures.

What kind of art went on the plane usually was the prerogative of the pilots, with the crew members having little input.

Miss Polk, 67, willed to a Memphis museum the scrapbooks containing love letters from her fiance, Col. Robert Morgan, the Memphis Belle pilot who, between bombing missions over German-occupied Europe during 1943, wrote his sweetheart, "I'll return to make you happy forever."

The happiness never happened. The two broke up during the pilot's highly publicized nationwide bond-selling tour. Miss Polk once told a university researcher that when she called the pilot at his hotel room one night a woman she didn't know answered the phone.

"That was it," she said. After a brief, unsuccessful marriage in the

1950s, she resumed her maiden name and lived most of her life single in Memphis.

I recently located Col. Morgan in Asheville, where he now lives with his third wife, Linda Dickerson of Illinois, also a pilot.

In May, the two will escort a 50th anniversary "Memphis Belle Remembered" tour to England.

I asked Col. Morgan how it feels to have something as personal as his love letters on public display.

"It doesn't bother me," he said. "That was a long time ago, and the letters are a part of history of that time."

He said he and Miss Polk had remained friends over the years.

In his biography of Walter Lippmann, author Ronald Steel mentioned Lippmann's affair with his best friend's wife, whom he later married.

Five of Lippmann's love letters to her in Europe, where she was on vacation, arrived after she sailed for home.

They were forwarded to her husband's business office in America. One was opened by his secretary, who sent it on to her boss.

This was a husband with class. He never opened the other four letters or even mentioned them to his wife. At his death, all five were found among his effects, along with a note: "For Helen, at my death."

Not every male is so chivalrous. Misplaced love letters can trigger firestorms of fury and grief.

I'm still convinced that, although they may make great reading in some future time, the wisest love letters are those written in the sand, taken out by the tide, yet remembered in the heart.

January, 1993

Adding up our great mistakes

In one of our many shopping centers, there is a store called "Great Mistakes." It sells clothes that are slightly flawed.

Somewhere in some sewing room, someone wasn't minding her needle and a garment had to be relegated to second-class status and sold at a discount.

All of us have made our "great mistakes." Fortunately, nobody rummages through our minds and holds them up for scrutiny. Except occasionally.

On a Sunday morning last fall I was browsing through the sports pages when my wife asked, "How did my little boy do?"

Her "little boy" was one of her students, a hulking member of the N.C. State football team. Usually, his name is there. So many yards. So many passes caught. Frequently a touchdown.

But on this particular Sunday morning, I had bad news for her. He had fumbled away the ball. And the game.

She was depressed. She thought she might tell him Monday morning that it didn't really matter. She would remind him that it was only a game. And only one game. And only one mistake. Think of all the times he hadn't made a mistake like that.

I urged her not to mention the fumble. Nobody needs to be reminded of his mistakes.

From the beginning of time, there have been great mistakes. If only Adam had said to Eve, "Woman, I never eat apples. All that fiber messes up my digestive system."

Or if Hitler had waited until spring to invade Russia. Or if only Napoleon, who suffered from hemorrhoids, had used Preparation H at Waterloo.

For many women, their great mistake was marrying the wrong man. I read that 79 percent of the women interviewed in a survey said they would not choose the same mate if given another go at marriage.

One of The News & Observer's great mistakes was a typographical error in an Under the Dome item during the administration of Gov. Luther Hodges. The governor, it said, was in the hospital "recuperating from a hernia received while lifting a widow at the Governor's Mansion."

A friend remembers when he bought a leisure suit — they were the rage in the '70s — and tried it on for his wife.

"You look just like an egg that the Easter Bunny overlooked," she said. He never put on the suit again.

One of my great mistakes was settling for a half-basement when we were building our house.

"But the contractor said he'd charge only $500 extra," my wife reasoned. (I know that's the correct figure because she often quotes it.)

"Five hundred dollars!" I had said. "Don't you realize our payments are already going to be $103.20 a month?" I was making $80 a week and the editor's job wouldn't be open for 18 years.

Athletes' mistakes somehow seem to be the best remembered.

Not long ago, our sports pages rehashed the University of South Carolina's 1971 ACC tournament upset of North Carolina. With seconds to go, it was jump ball. Ahead by one, UNC couldn't lose, with 6-10 Lee Dedmon jumping against 6-3 Kevin Joyce.

But the little guy outjumped the big guy and the Gamecocks won by one.

Lee Dedmon is now principal of Highland Junior High in Gastonia. Some years ago, while at another school, he was introduced by his principal to a UNC graduate who had come to deliver an address.

"This is Lee Dedmon," the principal said proudly, whereupon the visitor, a longtime Carolina fan with a longtime memory, blurted, "You didn't jump!"

Posted in the Great Mistakes store is a sign: "All Sales Final." Our human mistakes are usually final. But fortunately, most are forgettable. And forgivable.

And cheer up. Think of the great mistakes you never made.

April 1991

Choosing our sons-in-law

Ever since there were daughters, every father has wondered if there is a man out there good enough for his.

On the other hand, the mother of a male knows with certainty from the day of birth that no female on earth is worthy of her son.

I once ran into a friend who said his daughter seemed serious about a young man she was dating.

"I don't see how it can work out," he sighed. I asked why.

"He clips coupons," he said.

"That sounds very promising financially."

"It's not that kind of coupons," he replied. "He clips grocery coupons and saves them for double coupon day at the supermarket. And my daughter is the kind who thinks a cheap meal in a restaurant is one that starts at $20."

He was right. The romance wilted and died.

My friend admired the conservative streak in his daughter's boyfriend, but was wise enough to realize it could wreck the marriage down the road.

Another friend said he didn't want his child to marry a handsome man because other women would be trying constantly to steal him.

Most parents insist, "I just want whatever will make her (or him) happy." But that doesn't prevent them from harboring secret prerequisites.

Several years ago, I asked my own children what traits or characteristics they'd look for in a husband.

"He should be fun," one answered.

"What do you mean by 'fun'?"

"Fun to be with."

"Well, there is a difference," I explained. "It's tough being 'fun' when you don't know where the rent's coming from and the Master Charge is $1,000 in arrears."

I have always hoped that when a child of mine marries, it will be to someone with a pickup truck.

Today's young people are so mobile, a man can bring no greater dowry to his marriage than a vehicle capable of transporting their possessions.

My own two children have moved around so much in college and since that my dreams are constantly haunted by an orange U-Haul-It caught in 5 o'clock traffic on the approaches to Charlotte.

My older daughter once dated a fellow with a pickup. I liked the truck and the boy.

A quiet, unpretentious fellow, he didn't have much to say. But he knew how to lift a chest of drawers, and he always carried more than his share of the weight of a double mattress.

Alas, the relationship went on the rocks.

Later, when I asked why, she said, "He couldn't drive without a toothpick in his mouth. It had something to do with coordination."

"I wouldn't have cared if he chewed tobacco and carried a spit cup," I murmured in disappointment. "He had a pickup truck!"

At a Raleigh cocktail party for a distinguished author, a woman asked me who I would consider as a classic American author.

I mentioned Thomas Wolfe, aware that the woman, who was from Arkansas, might not appreciate Asheville's most famous son.

"I read his 'Look Homeward Angel' and didn't like it. It was too wordy," she said. She then told me how she came to read the novel in the first place.

"My daughter was at Vassar and was dating a boy at Princeton. She wrote to say that he really was into Thomas Wolfe's writing. So I read the book to see what kind of boy my daughter was dating."

"What kind of a boy was he?"

"Excellent! I liked the boy better than the book. He's been my son-in-law for over 20 years."

So, don't judge a boy by his book cover. Not long ago, I asked my own mother-in-law what she thought of me when first we met.

She paused for what seemed an eternity and then said icily, "I'd really rather not say. But I like you a lot now."

I courted her daughter in a Carolina-blue convertible. She might have liked me better had I come calling in a pickup truck.

March 1991

Billy Graham: wine or water?

To the folks in the foothills, the question was "Was it wine or was it water?"

The question related to the conduct of Rev. Billy Graham, probably the most beloved and trusted evangelist of our time.

For the faithful who have seen the likes of Jim Bakker bite the dust after succumbing to the sins of the flesh, Billy Graham is still the tree planted by the water, the tree that shall not be moved.

But then someone plants a small seed of doubt.

"I didn't see it on TV," my older sister, Zetta, said. "But my friend Inez told me that someone had told her that Dr. Graham drank a toast to President Clinton during the inauguration. She said he drank wine. But I doubt it."

"Is your friend a Republican?" I teased.

"What's that got to do with it?"

"Well, if your friend is a Republican, Billy Graham probably drank wine. Ask a Democrat, he'll say it was water."

"But what do you think?" my sister persisted. "I think it really doesn't matter. Not because of my politics, or because I don't think he should be criticized for drinking wine, if he indeed did. Remember how in the Good Book, the Lord changed water to wine? The Good Book doesn't say, touch not wine. It says, 'Be not drunk with wine.'"

"But the reason I think he drank water is that he would never knowingly confuse his flock by sipping the grape. Certainly not on TV in front of millions of his followers. That would be like drinking wine during one of his crusades."

My Baptist family abounds with teetotalers. Years ago, my nephew brought home a bottle of wine that a pretty French girl gave him during the Liberation of Paris.

His wife, Dot, although aghast at the idea of alcohol under her roof, was nevertheless sensitive to the gift's sentimental and historical significance. She buried the unopened bottle of wine at the bottom of her cedar hope chest.

In all probability, it's still there. And when she is gone to her heavenly reward, some neighbor will come in, go through her effects and, coming upon the wine, will exclaim, "Oh, dear, I never knew Dorothy drank!"

I asked my sister if she would love Dr. Graham less if he had indeed toasted the president with wine.

"Not really," she said. "But I would worry about his setting the wrong example."

Ah, there's the rub. People in high places, especially members of the cloth, must ever wear the weighty mantle of example setting.

A Raleigh friend, not concerned over whether the minister drank wine or water, instead was surprised that Dr. Graham prayed with his eyes open.

"Maybe he was reading from a TelePrompter," I suggested.

"Could be," she laughed. "But while my husband was saying grace at lunch that very day, I found myself with eyes wide open, watching a rufous-sided red-eyed towhee on my window feeder. And I didn't even feel guilty. Now that's the kind of influence the man has."

To lay the matter to rest and reassure the troubled, I put the question of whether it was wine or water to the White House media center and encountered my first "cover-up" of the new administration.

A young employee in the media center took two days to tell me that she couldn't find the answer to my question.

"It was an Inaugural Committee matter, and they won't return my calls," she finally concluded.

The Billy Graham headquarters at Montreat referred me to the Dallas, Texas, firm that handles the evangelist's public relations.

A Graham-gate? Not really. Only a tempest in a wine glass. But there will always be someone clutching a stone, eager to be the first to throw at a glass house.

So now, the envelope please, from Dr. Graham's Dallas spokesman.

"Dr. Graham drank water," he said. "He's always running into situations like that. And he always drinks water."

As for whether or not Dr. Graham prayed with his eyes open, I forgot to ask.

April 1993

It won't happen on a Monday!

Members of the "Reunion Committee" of the high school class that has never held a reunion were sitting around a table at a cafe in Dobson, planning the momentous event. We had had some difficulty just getting the committee together because of one conflict after another.

No, nobody had to prime tobacco. Or pick blackberries. Or go to a summer revival. It was a plethora of other things. Big things.

For one thing, Ida Johnsons's half-runners were coming in and she had to can beans. Betty Folger couldn't get away from Charleston because a grandchild was about to be born. I planned to attend a friend's retirement luncheon in Raleigh.

But there we were, finally, calendars in hand, choosing a date.

"How about Oct. 17?"

"Nope," John Norman said. "That's the weekend I close the vents under my house."

"I beg your pardon?" I asked, not trusting my ears.

"I said I close the vents under my house that weekend."

"You got a big house?"

"No, it's just something I do."

The incident illustrates how so many of us are slaves to our inflexibility.

When I was growing up, girls had a way of turning down dates by saying, "I'm so sorry, but I have to wash my hair that night."

A lot of women married the wrong men because they let dirty hair get in the way of an evening out at the Center Theatre, something small that might have turned into something big.

Some undoubtedly missed out on marriage altogether, but will go to their graves with clean hair. And some of you women might say, "Not a bad trade-off, really."

Judgment Day will never happen on Monday. You can take that to the bank. My neighbors, the Frank Smiths, wash on Monday. Her clean clothes flapping in the breeze provide comforting assurance that the Smiths will sleep on clean sheets for another week and the world will not end until Tuesday or later.

I am sure that somewhere in the Scriptures there is the Eleventh Commandment that says "Thou shalt wash on Monday."

I once overheard Annette, a friend of ours who teaches at the university, describing some early morning crisis with one of the children as the family was rushing about getting off to school.

"Thank goodness, it happened on a Wednesday, which is toast and cereal day," Annette sighed with relief. "I don't know what we would have done if it had happened on Tuesday or Thursday when we have bacon and eggs!"

Several years ago, while visiting my wife's relatives, plans were being made to call on a lovely lady with more money and time on her hands than she needed.

She insisted we visit. And soon! Somebody suggested the next Wednesday.

"Oh, no, my dears," she said, "Never on Wednesday. I dust my books on Wednesdays."

Even members of the world's oldest profession have the same phobia.

You no doubt remember the words of the catchy title song from the movie "Never on Sunday," in which Melina Mercouri plays the part of a hooker who adamantly sticks to her schedule:

"Oh you can kiss me on Monday, a Monday, a Monday is very, very good. Or you can kiss me on a Tuesday, a Tuesday, a Tuesday, in fact I wish you would.

"Or you can kiss me on a Wednesday, a Thursday, a Friday, and Saturday is best. But never, never on a Sunday, a Sunday, a Sunday, 'cause that's my day of rest."

The curse of inflexibility courses through every person's psyche. We just choose our own ground and to what degree we resist breaking a pattern.

My committee finally set Nov. 14 as the date for the first and last reunion of the Dobson High School class that had to graduate in the courthouse because somebody set the school on fire.

But I just remembered. I must check my calendar. That may be the weekend I'm supposed to rearrange my sock drawer.

August 1992

Seeking honest 4th graders

"Did your children ever steal?" I asked the mother of three adult children as we sat around drinking coffee.

"All children steal at one time or another," the mother replied.

In a Raleigh class, students were assigned to make a speech about some outstanding American. Several responded with Sandra Day O'Connor, Dr. Jonas Salk, Dr. Martin Luther King, etc. Then up popped Pete Rose.

"Really, I don't think Pete Rose is an acceptable role model," said the teacher.

"Well, why not? He's probably gonna make the Baseball Hall of Fame."

"But what about the gambling and income tax cheating? After all, he is in prison."

The students were adamant. Pete Rose is a folk hero.

"Don't you know," reasoned one student "that everybody cheats?"

Everybody cheats? Everybody steals?

Harvard University psychiatrist Robert Coles and Louis Genevie of Albert Einstein College of Medicine questioned 5,000 fourth- through 12th-graders on a number of moral dilemmas.

Twenty-one percent of elementary school kids freely admitted they'd try to copy answers from another student's test paper.

Kids from affluent homes had a greater tendency to be uncertain when faced with moral dilemmas than did poorer children.

The study also revealed that parents, worried about their children's self-image, encouraged them not to feel guilt or shame for their bad behavior.

As a child, I didn't steal. It wasn't that I was a goody-goody. It was fear, not of God's wrath but of my mother's, that kept me honest.

It was not until I was grown that I admitted to being an accomplice to the childhood theft of a chicken from my older sister's barnyard.

Her two sons and I, all about the same age, caught a big dominecker rooster and took him out to White's store, where we spent every last ounce of him on ice cream and candy.

We were never caught and punished. But I had to live with the guilt.

A Raleigh father recalls the time years ago when he and his two under-6 children visited the neighborhood drug store. That night, the younger child came to his bedroom, sobbing that she and her sister had each taken a piece of gum from an aisle display.

The father announced that the next day, after church, the two would pay for the gum and apologize to the manager.

Oh, no, they wept. A spanking would be more in order. Even a hard spanking. But these were non-spanking parents.

Next day, the tearful children each handed the manager a nickel and apologized.

The manager merely grunted.

No "Oh, that's all right," or "You're good scouts to come back and apologize." His brusqueness helped italicize the lesson.

Yes, most of us cheat, usually in small ways — a pen taken home from the office, an exaggerated mileage report, an extended lunch hour. Have you ever left a hotel with their towel?

Once, years ago, I coveted the towels in my Washington, D.C., hotel room. The ultimate in plush, they were in my favorite color of autumn gold. When I tried to buy them and could not, I was sorely tempted. I thought of respectable people I know who have bragged about their towel collections from hotels around the world.

But I knew that, while God would forgive me for taking the towel, my long-departed mother would not.

That's where honesty begins — in the home. Perhaps we should replace all the "Bless This House" needlepoint with "Thou Shalt Not Cheat."

And instead of raising up Pete Rose as the all-American hero, we need to tell kids about poor old Diogenes, who spent his life dragging his lantern about looking for an honest man.

What a tragedy it is that he's now reduced to looking for honest fourth-graders!

October 1989

A wife with 50 pairs of shoes!

A recent news story dealt with a local businessman who has fallen on hard times, having lost $12 million in business ventures. Included was a statement from the man's psychiatrist indicating that the man's wife once had, among other things, 300 pairs of shoes in her closets.

For many readers, the most interesting detail of this complex business catastrophe was a wife with 300 pairs of shoes.

It resurrected the image of Imelda Marcos fleeing the Philippines with her 3,000 pairs of footwear.

I have not counted the shoes in my wife's closet. But I know she does not accumulate them like baubles for an add-a-bead necklace. I'd guess she stocks fewer than a dozen pairs of wearable shoes.

As for me, I own six pairs, including my "yard shoes." Generally I alternate between two pairs, one brown, one black.

Many years ago, when I was making the world safe for democracy in the South Pacific, I was helping unload a jeep from one of our planes. When the guy opposite me dropped his half of the burden, the weight fell to me, crunching my back.

Now, switching shoes inevitably brings on bouts of "low back pain."

To a man afflicted by colorblindness, owning even two pairs of shoes can be troublesome.

More than once, having dressed in the predawn for my 7 a.m. job, I found myself at work wearing one brown and one black shoe.

This meant driving all the way home and changing. I finally discovered that you can go all day, attending any number of staff meetings and conferring with all kinds of important personages, without anyone noticing the mismatch.

Time was when her hat was a woman's glory. But hats went out of style years ago. Now, many women express themselves through their shoes, especially if they wear size 5.

No woman wearing size 7 or up is going to own 300 pairs of shoes.

Commenting on the Marcos footwear fiasco, Los Angeles Times columnist Jack Smith once mentioned in passing that his wife had 50 pairs of shoes. His readers were outraged.

"Why do you allow your wife to have 50 pairs of shoes?" one stormed. "Mrs. Marcos looted the public treasury to satisfy her vanity…her display of conspicuous consumption during widespread poverty is nauseating. She was this generation's Marie Antoinette. But in proportion, your wife exhibits the same conspicuous consumption.

"At the bottom of all this is a callous indifference to our fellow man-woman. In France, this indifference raged unchecked until the starving stormed the palace, chopped of Marie's head and paraded it around the streets."

You might ask the bankrupt Raleigh businessman the same question. But it may be that his wife, like mine, was reluctant to discard anything, and may have saved her shoes over a long period of time.

When I chide my wife for this character flaw, she reminds me of the many happy hours our two little girls spent clomping around in 3-inch heels held over from the '50s.

Some women express themselves with shoes. Others resort to "conspicuous consumption" via fur coats and BMWs. Show me a woman — or man, for that matter — who is totally free of a trace of ostentatiousness.

While my wife might spurn a fur coat or label 300 pairs of shoes as sheer excess, her extravagance runs to crystal and china.

At the Sermon on the Mount, if the good Lord had called for dinnerware on which to serve the loaves and fishes to the 5,000, my wife, had she been present, would have stood up and said, "I'll bring mine! I have just enough!"

Fortunately, nobody today is beheaded for reckless extravagances or "conspicuous consumption."

They lose their heads in other ways. Bankruptcy court has replaced the guillotine. For those accustomed to the grand lifestyle, I imagine it is almost as painful.

February 1993

A Madison County ending

Someone asked me not long ago if I could change the script of my life, would I alter it very much. I said probably not. I must have been having a good day that day.

For most of us, life has not been the great drama of which national best-sellers or Oscar-winning movies are made. Because we can't rewrite our own lives, it's fun to tinker with endings of other people's scripts.

A reader recently sent me an extremely clever piece by J. Douglas Bates, who has rewritten the ending of "The Bridges of Madison County."

Bates, a former managing editor of a Eugene, Ore., newspaper and the author of a couple of nonfiction books, has Robert Kincaid fleeing naked from the Iowa farm house under a hail of buckshot. More on that later.

I didn't like, "Scarlett," Alexandra Ripley's sequel to "Gone With the Wind," which made millions for her.

In fact, I thought my daughter, in the sixth grade at the time, did about as well with her own version of how GWTW should have ended.

At the end of my daughter's story, Rhett returned to a repentant Scarlett. And Ashley Wilkes, whom I always considered a wimp, hanged himself from one of the few trees the Yankees left standing at Twelve Oaks.

There are several chapters of the Bible I would rewrite, including Job and the parable of the Prodigal Son.

As a father, I'd probably imitate the biblical father by running out and throwing my arms around the returning son's neck, forgetting that he had left the farm at tobacco priming time to spend his inheritance on wine, women and song.

I identify too strongly with the hardworking brother who, returning on this particular day from the field, dog-tired and dirty, hears music and dancing up at the house.

When he asks what's going on, he is told, in effect, "Your Pa is celebrating the return of your no-count brother. They're having a pig pickin' and have hired the Smoky Mountain Boys string band for square dancing."

The resentful brother represents the unlovely reality of life, the downside of our disposition; the forgiving father is the epitome of our better self.

In what he calls 'The Britches of Madison County," Bates depicts the way the book would have ended in real life.

Francesca's husband returns unexpectedly to the farm and surprises his wife and the photographer in bed.

As he walks in, Francesca is explaining that she can't accept her lover's invitation to come away from the farm with him.

"Don't you see, I love you so much that I cannot think of restraining you for a moment. To do that would be the kill the wild, magnificent animal that is you."

Shotgun in hand, the enraged husband shouts, "'That's all right, Frannie. I'm going to kill the wild, magnificent son-of-a-bitch myself.'

"Francesca Johnson let out a shriek, and Robert Kincaid, moving with the physical grace of an animal, possibly a jackrabbit, hopped off the bed and crouched behind it.

"Richard, swift as the prairie wind, took three big steps toward him and tried to lift him off the floor by his handsome, long, silver-gray tresses, but the hairpiece came off in Richard's grasp, and he tossed it aside with disgust."

Meanwhile, Francesca is pleading that there is an explanation, while Robert Kincaid "slowly rose, bravely, gracefully like a Labrador retriever, wearing nothing except the silver chain around his neck. 'I am the highway and a peregrine,' he began, 'and all that sails that—'.

"'Ah, shove it!' Richard Johnson said, angrily pumping a shell into the chamber of the shotgun. 'You'd better hit that highway out there by the count of 10, Mr. Peregrine, or I'll put a load of birdshot into your bony behind. One. Two. Three...'"

Anyway, in Bates' version, Kincaid, his Levis in his hands, flees in his pickup truck, knocking down the mailbox as he goes. And Francesca is looking at her husband in a new light.

"He grunted and turned away, moving like a powerful animal — a Hereford bull, actually. 'Think I'll catch the late livestock report. Any of the Budweiser left?'

"He headed downstairs. She lit another Camel. The corn grew."

I think the book probably would have ended that way if it had been set in in bloody Madison County in Western North Carolina, instead of tranquil Madison County in central Iowa.

That's the difference in real life and fiction. But sometimes it's those beautiful, heart-tugging fictional endings that help ease us through the grim chapters of the reality that is life.

November 1993

God doesn't play basketball

As far as I'm concerned, the Old Reliable could omit the sports section between April and September.

For me, baseball is the national "boretime." I've never understood why people doze for hours in front of a televised stock car race, awakening occasionally to hope for a crash into the wall or at least a wheel spinoff to break the monotony.

As for golf, I agree with one of columnist Mike Royko's readers, who said:

"This is a sport? These people are dressed in street clothes. They are never out of breath. Some of them are wearing saddle shoes. They have servants to carry their equipment."

College basketball is my bag. And to tell you the truth, after such a strenuous season, even I'm ready for a rest.

And so, I imagine, is God.

You didn't know God played basketball? Well, I didn't think so either. But apparently I'm in a minority.

On the day before Duke played Arkansas for the national championship, two friends, one a lawyer, the other a minister, sent me scurrying to the Bible for evidence that the Devils were going to carve up the Hogs.

There it was in Mark 5:13 and Matthew 8:31-32:

"...And the unclean spirits went out and entered into the swine; and the herd ran violently down a steep place into the seas, and they were choked in the sea."

Well, unfortunately, the "unclean spirits" prevailed by four points.

I don't know what prompted God to go with the Hogs.

I do know that when the Blue Devils, score tied, returned to the floor for the second half, Coach Mike Krzyzewski sat down and immediately crossed himself.

"Uh-oh! Coach K's gone to the Lord!" chuckled one of the sports announcers.

And the way underdog Duke bellied up to those "unclean spirits" right up to the final buzzer almost made a convert of me.

The Rev. Jerry Falwell let it be known even before Liberty University's tip-off with heavily favored Carolina that he thought God was on his side.

According to the experts, Liberty had a 10 trillion to one chance of beating No. 1 ranked Carolina.

"We have no intention of losing," said Mr. Falwell, the school's founder, just before the game. "This isn't just for us and the university.

We want to reflect well on the Lord. If you're a Christian you want to do well for the Lord."

Liberty's coach echoed the ecclesiastical optimism by saying that when you're attacking against Goliath, you need to be plugged into the "Ultimate Source," the ultimate source being the Lord.

Again, I was almost convinced that God truly had entered the fray when the Heels trailed from time to time before their eventual 20-point win. But to think that the lopsided loss reflected poorly on the Lord is pure hogwash!

I like the way UNC Coach Dean Smith, a good Baptist, addresses the business of God's sports participation in Thad Mumau's book, "Dean Smith: a Biography."

"People depend on sports when they don't have the inner affirmation of security or success," Smith said. "When we won the national championship in '82, we were flooded with letters saying God willed that the kid (Fred Brown of Georgetown) throw the ball to James (Worthy.) That's the same mentality that God was on our side during World War II."

You mean, he wasn't, Coach?

Obviously, many people involve God in even the most minute decisions of life.

I once sat astonished while a relative described how, a few days earlier, she had been running late for her hair appointment.

"I just knew I wasn't going to make it," she said. "But then I asked God to turn all the stoplights green in my favor. He did and I got there just on the dot!"

To me, this was the height of vanity, bordering on blasphemy. God is not a traffic engineer and, even if he were, why would he favor someone heading to a hair appointment over, say, an ambulance rushing a heart attack victim to a hospital?

But she is no worse than two senior citizens in a Raleigh restaurant who, having finished their meal, asked the waiter, an acquaintance of ours, to fetch the dessert tray.

The two women hemmed and hawed over the choices, citing the merits of the chocolate eclair as opposed to the blueberry cheesecake.

Finally, one said to her companion,"Well, dear, which one do you think Jesus would choose?"

Personally, I try not to spend whatever green stamps I may have with God on such trivia as choosing desserts, barber shop appointments — and yes, not even on college basketball. I try to save my credits for life's real crises.

May 1994

Watching the liver bleed

I can't help clinging to the idea that Raleigh is still a small town, even though North Carolina's Capital City has grown so fast you'd think a plane had flown over and sprayed the place with Miracle Gro.

Its rampaging growth has created a problem for those of us who won't let go of the concept that although the population is changing drastically, the lifestyle shouldn't.

I, for one, am constantly butting heads with the reality of change, as I did last week at a branch bank where I cashed a comparatively small check from the Old Reliable.

"I'll need some identification," said the young woman behind the counter.

"It's a payroll check, and I've been banking with you folks for 40 years," I sighed unhappily, reaching for my wallet and my IDs.

"Does anyone know this man?" the woman suddenly yelled to the other cashiers along the line. I cringed as all eyes turned my way.

Finally, another cashier, talking to someone on the telephone, nodded her head in the affirmative. The check was promptly cashed.

The incident reminded me of an unforgettable line from the movie "Terms of Endearment." A mother, grocery shopping with two restless kids, came up short at the checkout line.

"This woman says she doesn't have enough money to pay for her groceries!" the cashier bellowed across the store to the manager.

As the victim winced with embarrassment, the man in line behind her said angrily to the cashier, "You must be from New York!"

"You must be from New York," I said to the teller as she handed me my money.

"I am," she said, surprised. "How did you know?"

"Your name," I lied, indicating her placard. "It's not a local name. It's New Yorkish."

A Raleigh friend, gift in hand and observing small-town protocol, called on a young couple who had recently moved to her street. She knocked and knocked before the door was finally cracked by a young woman who said brusquely, "I don't know you!" and slammed the door.

When my friend described the incident to her 91-year-old mother, her mother said "Honey, I have told you time and time again to stay away from Yankees."

"But Mother, I understand the woman went to Sweetbriar," explained her daughter.

"Well, dear, Sweetbriar has gone way down in recent years," her mother sighed.

Her South Carolina born and bred mother was passing on a prejudice drilled into her by her own parents. Throughout her childhood, they had cautioned her to "stay away from Yankees."

"I remember longing to just see how one looked," her mother recalled. "Finally, a milliner from somewhere up north moved to town. She seemed perfectly normal. But remember, my dear, I never saw a Republican until I married your Daddy and moved to Elkin."

I had a welcome sampling of small-town charm last week when I met my friends Dick and Nita Byrd for our customary country ham breakfast at the Riverside Restaurant in Mount Airy.

The Byrds moved to the hills a few years ago and bought and restored a beautiful 150-year-old home at the foot of the mountain. Although the Byrds are still considered "newcomers," several people came by our table to chat.

I met Jim Davis, a University of Tennessee graduate, who, when I complained about my faltering Tar Heels, pointed out that his Volunteers have won only five games all season.

Jim had just finished removing from his lawn a shrub that had become a mote in his wife's eye.

"I tied one end of a rope around the shrub's base and the other end to the bumper of my car and gave it the gun. The rope broke. I tried two ropes, which also broke. The same thing with three ropes. I finally attacked the shrub's roots with a mattock, while my wife kept reminding me that I had had two heart bypasses and there was no need to tempt fate. But I noticed that she never outright ordered me to stop as she does when I mention playing golf."

Nita gestured to a couple at an adjoining table.

"Now there's a wonderful couple. He is such a thoughtful husband. It's his second marriage and he had a vasectomy reversal so she could have children."

The bulge under the woman's maternity dress testified to the operation's huge success.

To our left, five look-alike, past-50 women wearing jogging outfits chatted happily.

"They call themselves the Hoof and Mouth Club," Nita explained. "They say they mouth more than they hoof."

WPTF's Maury O'Dell recently described a small town as a place where, for excitement, you go down to the service station and watch them do a lube job or go to the meat market to watch the liver bleed.

Well, I want more excitement than that in my town. But not a whole lot more.

February 1994

The dean spins in her grave

When I was a student at Chapel Hill, men outnumbered women 7,000 to 800. Considering my handicaps as a Casanova, I was indeed fortunate to be able to call on a young grad student by the name of Phyllis Gentry, who lived in Kenan Dorm.

If sometimes I wandered from the "parlour" down the hall toward her room, a cry would go up "Man on the hall!" Dean Catherine Carmichael would come running and escort me out the front door.

Last week, UNC officials, by a vote of students and a stroke of a pen, converted Kenan and five other dorms from one-time havens of propriety into Houses of Cohabitation.

And in Heaven, Dean Carmichael is tugging at God's sleeve, pointing Chapel Hillward, and sighing, "Look, Lord! What next?"

University officials gave students a vote on whether to have legitimate sex in the dorms or just keep sleeping around behind the chancellor's back. It's no great surprise that 84 percent voted to do it in the dorm. It's like asking 5-year-olds if they'd like ice cream three times a day.

Just like parents who have lost control over their children, university officials have no problem justifying their action.

They sound like a fellow in the foothills who outraged my churchgoing relatives by allowing his 16-year-old daughter's boyfriend to move into his house.

"Well," the neighbor drawled in self-defense. "I figger they gonna do it anyway, and it's a heap better and safer for them to do it in the next room rather than on the back seat of his car up behind the community college."

And a great deal more comfortable, he could have added.

It may indeed be wiser to have Carolina students doing it within the comparative safety of a dorm room rather than out there on the ground in the Arboretum, where they might catch their death of cold or be murdered by passing psychopaths.

I don't know if the university will be legally liable for the prenatal care, diapers and day care of babies conceived under university sponsorship. Even if it is, the taxpayers will be footing the bill, as they do in almost every case of irresponsible parenthood.

We have to admit that the university is putting first things first: safe and comfortable sex and a winning program in basketball and football.

The least the university can do is stock the dorm rooms with free condoms, even in the face of disturbing news from the British Medical

Journal, which recently reported that the standard failure rate for preventing pregnancy by condoms is from 15 to 20 percent.

Atlanta Journal columnist Dick Williams presents an interesting analogy that residents of Carolina's free-sex dorms might keep in mind:

"If you were invited to go skydiving with five friends, then told that one of the parachutes would fail, would anyone jump? Or even get on the plane?"

Williams makes a point. But five guys jumping out of a plane with one parachute not opening is better than five guys jumping without wearing a parachute at all.

It's true that sex in the dorm room is nothing new.

When my elder daughter checked in at Carolina almost a decade ago, we were impressed by her lovely roommate from Fort Worth, Texas.

But the relationship soon soured as, night after night, my daughter came home from studying at the library to find herself locked out of her room and her roommate's lover locked in. That first semester, the guy spent almost as many nights in the room as my daughter did.

A friend's freshman daughter fared worse. She kept calling home to complain that, even though she put a pillow over her head to shut out the noises from the next bed, she couldn't get any sleep when her roommate's boyfriend — a married Romeo from Fayetteville — slept over a couple of nights a week.

A telephone call to the roommate cleared up the problem: Cut out the cohabitation or the man's wife would be notified pronto that her traveling salesman hubby, instead of curling up with a good book in a lonely motel, was curling up with a cute coed in a Chapel Hill dorm room.

University officials are not without compassion. If a roommate doesn't like the conjugal arrangement, they will try to find the unhappy roomie another home.

Here we go again: It's the "victim" who'll be moved.

The headline on the sex dorms story asks: What will mom and dad say about this?

"Thank God, my Tommy is living at the fraternity house and not in one of those dorms!" sighed one sanctimonious mother. The survey ended right there.

All this is sour grapes on my part, you say. Maybe. I was born a bit too soon. But in this case, university officials were born a bit too foolish.

September 1993

Killing doesn't make a man

I did not see Steven, my 11-year-old great-nephew, during the Thanksgiving holidays. He stayed in Virginia to go deer hunting with his dad.

"Has he killed one yet?" I asked his mother.

"No," she sighed. "He hadn't when I left home. I hope he still hasn't."

She is sensitive to her son's inner conflicts. He is a very intelligent, quiet and sensitive lad. She suspects that deep inside, compassion is wrestling with reality.

Reality is being born into a community and a family where men almost instinctively take to hunting. The boy enjoys the outdoors and the camaraderie with his father, who is an avid hunter.

Killing animals is a matter of macho. Killing the first deer will be the boy's bar mitzvah to manhood.

"I know it won't be easy," his mother said of the impending moment when Steven, a deer in his gun sights, will muster the will to squeeze off the trigger.

His mother told how he came home one day after being in the woods alone. Lying down to rest, he had fallen asleep, only to be awakened by a deer nibbling at a nearby bush.

At home, he got down on his all-fours to show his mother how the deer walked in that awkward tiptoe that gives way to a ballerina's grace and beauty when the deer takes flight.

Steven likes to sketch. Not long afterward, he sketched a deer, a deer with tears coursing down its face.

The boy's first kill may well bring the same kind of trauma that another hunter, Lemuel T. Ward, experienced when he fired into a flock of geese, bringing down two of the wild birds.

In a poem, recently printed by Ann Landers, Ward describes how the male bird lay on the beach moaning piteously as its wounded mate dragged her body to his side, covered him with a broken wing, laid her head against his breast and died.

Ward buried the birds in the sand, wrapped in his hunting coat. On the way home, he threw his gun and belt into the bay.

"Hunters will call me a right poor sport and scoff at the thing I did.

But that day something broke in my heart, and shoot again? God forbid."

I had my fill of hunting when I was a boy of 5 or 6. When my older brothers returned from the woods with the rabbit and the squirrel, my distasteful chore was holding the dead animals by their back legs while they were being skinned.

I still remember winter mornings when, glad to be going, I went off to school with the echo of gunfire in my ears as the annual slaughter of hogs got under way.

Hunters say there is something exciting and unforgettable about the first kill. Hunters say that once you have killed your first wild thing, killing comes easier.

That seems to be the way with killing in general. In a culture that feeds on violence on TV, on our highways, in Bosnia and elsewhere, where teenage terrorists machine gun women and children like so many beer cans lined atop a fence, the killing apparently comes easy indeed.

The killer instinct lurks in varying degrees within us all. Notice how, after smearing the quarterback, the linebacker, his fists slicing the air, leaps and twists in spontaneous spasms of ecstasy.

See how, after he has clobbered his opponents in the TV debate, the politician struts off the stage.

Even a newspaper editor kills — with his volley of verbs, adjectives, nouns and punctuation marks — fired into the heart of a crooked officeholder or an out-of-control bureaucrat.

I called my niece after the Thanksgiving holiday.

"Did Steven kill his first deer?"

"Not yet," she said. "But I know it's inevitable."

Maybe not. Maybe someone will let the boy know that times have changed. He no longer has to kill to be a man.

December 1992

Two-minute eggs and speeches

Dean Richard Cole ought to run for public office. He has come up with the best idea since sliced bread.

The head of the University of North Carolina's School of Journalism and Mass Communication recently introduced a new wrinkle in public speaking by limiting to two minutes the acceptance speeches of inductees into the North Carolina Journalism and Advertising Halls of Fame.

Worrying about over-run, I almost took along my wife's kitchen timer for the occasion. I use the timer in preparing two of only three dishes in my culinary repertoire. One is a two-minute egg, the other 15-minute long-grain Comet rice.

I reminded the audience that, thanks to Dean Cole, they were getting the two-minute egg speech.

Think of what such a limit on rhetorical bombast could do for politicians. It could actually endear them to the public as well as to their peers. It could substantially speed up lawmaking and practically wipe out foot-in-mouth disease.

Every public performance seems to wear on far too long these days.

At concerts, no matter how good or bad the performance, there are always standing ovations, which lead to innumerable encores. It's come to the point that you can now expect a standing ovation at a tractor pull at the State Fairgrounds.

Sure, it's rude to leave during the encore. But a lot of folks do it. I just hang on, thinking about what a pain it's going to be getting out of the parking lot.

At least I'm honest about it. I'm not like the man I sat next to at a Friends of the College concert. On his feet, clapping wildly, he was yelling, "Bravo! Bravo!" at the top of his voice, meanwhile hissing to his wife out of the side of his mouth, "Get your coat on, honey!"

Worse than over-long concerts are over-long speeches. I can count on one hand the number of speeches that I wished would last longer than they did. The vast majority of orations, including President Clinton's, could be cut by half with no harm done.

Consider the length of Lincoln's Gettysburg address — 135 words. In Genesis, it took only 10 words to tell of the Creation: "In the beginning, God created the heaven and the earth."

On the other hand, President William Henry Harrison's inaugural address rambled on for 9,000 words, delivered in the face of a freezing northeast wind. The long-winded Harrison came down with a cold next day and died of pneumonia a month later. Served him right.

Have you ever heard of anyone complaining that a speech was too short? Of course not.

Civic clubs are the worst offenders. I had to give up Rotary because when I was a full-time editor I couldn't sacrifice two hours each Monday to the club's good works and speechmaking.

CBS news anchor Dan Rather, in a speech to newspaper editors, once recalled the time when, as a young man working on a Houston radio station, he was invited to speak to the Houston Lions Club.

After spending long hours polishing his speech, he showed up early for the momentous occasion. The program droned on and on until at 1:30 p.m., the presiding Lion tapped his water glass and, instead of introducing Rather, said abruptly, "Well, that's it, Lions. Roar!"

When a stunned Rather walked up, he said, "Oh. You. Well, we did not quite get to it this week, maybe some other time. OK?"

Not to be denied his one opportunity to speak at the prestigious Rice Hotel, Rather strode to the rostrum and began delivering his speech, amid the clatter of dishes being cleared by the kitchen crew.

He was four paragraphs into it when he noticed, sitting in the shadows along the wall, a local newspaper columnist named Morris Frank.

"Mr. Frank, you have no idea how much I appreciate your staying here to hear me speak," Rather said humbly. "But it's not necessary."

"Oh, hell, get on with it!" snapped Mr. Frank. "I am the next speaker."

Brevity in most things is to be admired. Even the Bible agrees: "Let thy speech be short, comprehending much in a few words."

A two-minute egg is tolerable; a three-minute egg is too hard to intake. So it is with speeches.

April 1993

'If Mama ain't happy'

In a downtown Raleigh store, one T-shirt in a window display stands out: 'If Mama ain't happy, ain't nobody happy!'

Truer words were never spoken.

Without intending to sound sexist, I am convinced that from the cradle to the grave, men feel the necessity to keep the women in their lives happy. And well they should.

A woman has so many duties, so many responsibilities and her influence is so inclusive that her mood can make or break a day for an entire family.

And if she is a teacher, she can spoil it for 30 to 40 kids and their families. If she is an executive, she can louse up the day for whoever is under her command.

This is not to say that a mean and moody father never casts an uncomfortable shadow across the dinner table.

But in the majority of homes and offices, it is the female who not only creates the turbulent tides but also calms the restless waves.

In sports, when the TV camera scans the stands, the signs always read "Hi, Mom!" Never, ever "Hi, Dad!"

Even in pro games, after some hulk scores a touchdown or intercepts a pass, the big lummox usually mouths "Hi, Mama!" into the camera.

Earlier this year, Raleigh's Dr. Assad Meymandi wrote me about the death of his mother at age 101. In the letter, he noted that "mothers are saints."

He pointed out that in moments of stress, it's Mom, not Dad, we turn to. He noted that when Napoleon Bonaparte was captured in Russia, he cried, "ou estu, mama?"... i.e., "Mother, where are you?"

When a weeping Richard Nixon went before a TV audience of 100 million people to say goodbye as he left the White House in disgrace, he said through his tears, "My mother was a saint."

Recently, in Wake Superior Court, when the judge reprimanded a woman for talking aloud, the young defendant overturned a table and yelled, "You can't talk to my mama like that!"

Over the years, when our children called from college or elsewhere and I answered the phone, their first question would be, "How's Mother?"

And Mother had better be in a good mood.

Occasionally my wife would answer the phone only to hear "Mother, what's wrong? You sound down?"

"I'm not 'down,' I'm tired," she would say, since she's usually a very "up" person.

But she got the message: 'Mother, don't you dare be 'down.' It depresses us kids." When Mom is "down," the world somehow is out of kilter.

During the nomination process of Supreme Court nominee Ruth Bader Ginsburg, columnist Calvin Trillin reported that Judge Ginsburg laughs so rarely that her daughter actually wrote down the occasions as a child and put them together for a book to be called "Mommy Laughs."

My mother rarely laughed. But the Holders were known for their reserve. Also, a smile can be disarming. When you're the mother of several sons, you can't let your guard down, even for a moment.

Check out the art museum. Mona Lisa's mere suggestion of a smile inspired a song that has survived the decades.

In his most famous work, Whistler endowed his mother with an expression as cheerful as a funeral in a sleet storm.

Mama's role today is more crucial than ever.

A strong Mama can chart a course for her children that will surmount incredible obstacles. Consider the case of a vocational student in the Winston-Salem schools.

"I can't stand this mortar," complained the 6-foot-4 student in a bricklaying course. "It messes up my hands. I gotta have some gloves."

The instructor explained that a bricklayer has to have the feel of the brick in order to do the job right. Laying bricks with gloves on is like Paderewski playing the piano in mittens.

When Maurice didn't show for class for several days, the instructor called his mother, who thanked him for the call.

Next morning, Maurice was in class. Behind him, perched on a stool, was his tiny mother, about five feet tall.

"Now what is it you want Maurice to do?" she asked. The instructor led the young man to a stack of bricks.

"Maurice, do what the man says, you heah?" Mama ordered.

Maurice heard. And did. Maurice graduated from bricklaying with honors. No 18-year-old wants his mama sitting behind him anywhere — least of all in the classroom.

Responding to a column on sibling rivalry, a Salter Path reader wrote that she sometimes believes that mothers are often the instigators of sibling rivalry, "so that all the children will love her first, rather than each other.

"After all, she deserves some compensation for her labors and trials. Also, the 'kids' compete for the parent's affection. Each wants to be first in line for love rationed out by Mama."

Happy Mother's Day — Mom, Mama, Mother.

May 1994

Catching last bus to Heaven

Have you noticed that your preacher hasn't dwelt on Hell much lately? The new thing in the ministry is to accentuate the positive — Heaven — and de-emphasize the negative — Hell.

When I was growing up — fear of the dark, fear of my parents and the fear of a fire and brimstone Hell — made me the good boy I was.

I have just come across an old Andy Rooney column pointing out that the scientific exploration of space has complicated religion's position on good and evil, eternal reward and damnation. Hell is definitely being de-emphasized.

"Now that we've been to the moon, kids aren't afraid of going to Hell anymore and you can't do a thing with them," said Mr. Rooney.

"You don't hear people say 'up in Heaven' anymore. Science has turned 'up' into 'out,' and research by the oil companies has destroyed any concept we had of Hell, because if it were down there, they'd have found it and discovered a way to make a profit of it."

Come to think of it, I don't recall ever threatening my kids with Hell. And their only concept of the devil was the guy who, dressed in dark blue, danced around with a pitchfork in the end zone at the Duke-Carolina game.

But I did tell them about Heaven. And, of course, they came up with their own version of what Heaven should be. Don't we all?

A reader has sent me a copy of a study conducted several years ago by U.S. Catholic Magazine on how Catholics view Heaven and Hell.

Eighty-six percent believe there is a Hell, but 84 percent surveyed said God doesn't send anyone there. People, by their actions, choose to go there.

Most of those surveyed discount Hell as a roaring inferno, but believe that real Hell is the absence of God.

Like Protestants, most no longer cling to the idea of Heaven as an urban setting with streets of gold.

I, too, prefer to think of Heaven as rural, free of shopping centers and Crabtree Valley traffic jams, replete with endless green pastures, babbling brooks and April-May weather. And there has to be great groves of dogwood.

A Gary, Ind., sports fan said, "In Heaven, we'd play lots of baseball. In the seventh game of the celestial series, I'd hit one of God's fast balls into the upper deck to win the game and the series."

I like sports, but I hope Heaven is not another Dean Dome. I'd like a good library, a clean beach and a decent coffee shop where I could endlessly shoot the bull with friends, knowing I didn't have to hurry home to mow the yard or clean the gutters.

I've never heard a sermon on sex in Heaven. But the Catholic survey noted that, although men and women will retain their sexuality in Heaven, marriage and procreation will not exist there.

That's just as well, considering all the sexual hang-ups on Earth, the prevalent divorce rate and multiple marriages.

I wouldn't envy God's having to decide which of Liz Taylor's seven husbands would share her cloud in Paradise.

The survey notes that when U.S. Catholic readers arrive in Heaven they will, in this order, (1) hug God, (2) find relatives who have died before them and (3) ask God some tough questions, including "Why did you create mosquitoes?"

That sounds normal. Except the third thing I'd do would be to look up Peter and tell him how deeply I identified with him when I read about the cock crowing thrice.

Heaven sounds wonderful. Always has. And, yes, I want to go. But I'm like the fellow who kept his seat when the preacher asked those in the congregation who wanted to go to Heaven to stand up.

Confronted, the fellow explained, "Oh, I thought you meant now. Of course I want to go — but preferably on the last bus."

August 1991

'You're not listening, dear'

Deborah Tannen, professor of linguistics at Georgetown University, says in a Washington Post article that the inability of men and women to talk to each other has a lot to do with one of every two marriages going on the rocks.

She says women tell men, "You aren't listening," and the men protest, "I am!"

The man is right, she says. It's just that the mechanics of the conversation is deceiving.

Her research shows that when women talk, they face each other across the table, with their eyes anchored on each other's faces.

"At every age, boys and men sat at angles to each other and looked elsewhere in the room, periodically glancing at each other."

One young woman complained to Ms. Tannen that whenever she tries to talk to her boyfriend, he lies down on the floor, closes his eyes and puts his arm over his face.

"This signaled to her, 'He's taking a nap.' But he insisted he was listening extra hard," Ms. Tannen concluded.

I say men and women from the beginning of time have always sent mixed messages and will never understand each other entirely. They were designed that way.

One of my friends and his wife headed out early one morning on a vacation trip.

Breezing along U.S. 1 near Richmond, he asked cheerfully, "Honey, where do you want to stop for breakfast?"

"Oh, anywhere, dear" she replied sweetly.

"No, pick out a place," he insisted, as they were passing along a strip of eateries.

"I told you. Anywhere will be just fine," she said, a little irritably.

He wheeled into the parking lot of a waffle shop.

"We're going to eat here?" she asked in surprise.

"Yeah, you said anywhere."

Inside, they ordered waffles. After all, it was a waffle shop.

The waitress brought the waffles, golden brown. They tasted great.

"But then that confounded cockroach crawled from under my wife's waffle," he recalled, with a sigh. "Its legs were dripping syrup, but it labored stickily up the side of the waffle, and plodded sluggishly but courageously across the top of it while my wife watched in horror."

Yelling for the waitress, the poor husband pointed to the weary cockroach.

"Oh, dear," the girl sighed as she removed the plate. "We sprayed for the damn things just last night. I guess one got away."

"When we walked back to the car, my wife didn't say a word. She didn't have too," my friend recalled. "The way she held her head and the 'You screwed up again' expression on her face said it all."

It happens all the time. A couple who can agree on almost every detail of building a house, buying a new car or raising a family can come close to divorce when deciding where they will go for dinner.

But women are more sensitive than men. Thank God.

Ms. Tannen interviewed a woman who underwent surgery for removal of a lump from her breast. She was particularly upset because the operation changed the contour of the breast. Her girlfriend sympathized, "You feel like your body has been violated."

But her practical husband only said, "You can have plastic surgery to restore the shape of your breast."

The friend was comforting and reassuring. But not the husband who complained that he didn't like the contour of the breast.

I'm a good listener where women are concerned. They're usually interesting. For better or worse, they are more apt to get at the root of human emotions. They like to probe the psyche, dangerous though that may be.

Men, less revealing, tend to discuss their golf scores or sexual exploits — or lack of them. That's the way they've been taught to be. Still, men are easier to read, at least easier for other men to read.

But any man stupid enough to lie on the floor with his face covered while a woman is addressing him surely deserves the grief that's headed his way.

July 1990

Fish more, make love less

How the mighty hath fallen!
Listen to this lament from Gen. Norman Schwarzkopf: "Seven months ago, I could give a single command and 541,000 people would immediately obey it. Today I can't get a plumber to come to my house."
Now the general knows how the rest of us feel.

A Raleighite says that when he recently called a plumber's office, the receptionist wanted to know who was calling.

"And what is the problem?" she asked after he identified himself.

"It's the commode. It's stopped up."

"Well, really, Mr. Ponder is quite busy. Let me see. He could get to you maybe the second Tuesday in March."

"This is ridiculous," said my friend. "Let me speak to him."

"He's with a patient — er, I mean, client. Actually we aren't taking on new clients. I'll be glad to recommend..."

"But he's been my plumber for 20 years, ever since my wife dropped her wristwatch down the commode!"

"Well, I'll speak to him," said the receptionist reluctantly.

In a moment she was back. "You're in luck. Mr. Ponder has had a cancellation. You can bring the commode in tomorrow afternoon at 3:30."

That's what it has come to, folks. It's tragic enough for a town to lose its only doctor. Just wait until all our plumbers pass on and all we have left are people who majored in Interpersonal Communications and know absolutely nothing about how to unstop the sink or replace the ball in the commode tank.

I have always admired those people who can make miracles happen with their hands — no matter what their specialty. In a society sick with pretension and artificiality, it's refreshing to spend time with straightforward plain-talking people.

This week I watched as a couple of lumberjacks made quick work of cutting up a couple of trees for me. I envied the brute strength and marveled at the furious pace and, yes, the certain grace, with which one of the men attacked the big oak logs.

When he paused to rip apart a reluctant half-split log with his bare hands, I said, "Fellow, you work so hard; what do you do for fun?"

Straightening his back, he turned with a grin and said, "Make love and fish. Fish and make love."

"Yeah, he's got five kids under 10," his partner said sarcastically. "He ought to fish more and make love less."

Neither one of my children went into the trades, an oversight I sometimes regret.

I remember when Melinda, my eldest, called home from Carolina to say that she had just gone through a battery of career aptitude tests.

"Daddy, you'll never guess what they say I'm best suited for," she said mysteriously.

"Medicine?" I asked hopefully.

Every father covets a child with a medical background and the accompanying financial security to see him through his sunset years.

"Nope. Guess again."

"Not newspapering. I've told you. No more newspapering in this family."

"You'll never guess," she said. "According to the test results, I'm best suited to be a priest — or rather a priestess."

"I forbid it!" I said. "Go in another door and take the tests again. Maybe they misread the results and you're supposed to be a psychiatrist, which is a lot like being a priest, except the pay is fantastic and you don't have to be 'called.'"

Almost totally dependent on machines, we are now at the mercy of a group of people who never went to college to study mass communications or medicine. They are the people who work with their hands.

There is a certain poetic justice in whatever arrogance they may choose to display.

For they know very well that on a cold, winter night when the bathroom is flooded and we call the plumber, the sweetest words under the cope of Heaven is "Mr. Ponder is on his way."

November 1991

Wee lads with 'girl problems'

It is 7:30 on a sunny May morning. Swinging down the path in the wooded neighborhood park where I take my walk came two boys — "wee lads," my Scottish friend Al Edwards would say.

Slinking along at a safe distance was a gray-striped cat, curiously and irresistibly drawn to the sense of swaggering adventure that only little boys on an outing together can know.

"We caught a crawdad in the creek yesterday!" one said excitedly. "We're going back to catch some more!"

Chattering happily, the two boys looked as if they might have walked off the pages of "Tom Sawyer" or "Huckleberry Finn." Except for one thing.

I was flattered that they dared share their excitement with me — a stranger. But they felt quite safe. After all, unlike Tom and Huck, they were "armed."

One carried a .22 type "rifle," the other a rapid-fire piece. Toys, of course.

The sight of two little boys with guns might not have hit me as hard had I not just read a newspaper article by a young journalist by the name of Adam Smith. He wrote about the suicide of an 11-year-old Spartanburg, S.C. boy.

It was another one of those tragic, heartbreaking cases in which an outwardly happy youngster who has everything suddenly decides he has nothing, and puts a gun to his head.

I was especially drawn to two bits of information in the well-written piece.

The death weapon, a .12-gauge shotgun, had been a gift to the boy.

And Jimmy recently had suffered "a misunderstanding with his girlfriend."

Eleven years old? Girl problems? Shotguns?

So much, so soon.

Who among us has not, at one time or another, entertained the fleeting thought that life isn't worth living? With an instrument of death easily available, many more might have done what this youngster did.

But the young are especially vulnerable.

Novelist Jessamyn West once recalled that in grade school she had written an essay on "Live life deeply!" Her insensitive teacher had reprimanded her in front of the whole class for her exuberance.

Driven by her classmates' teasing and taunts, she decided to end it all.

"The only way a young lady could do away with herself in those days was by drowning in a pool," she wrote. "But in Whittier there were no pools deep enough. Then I remembered the reservoir up above town.

"I sent my white skirt to the cleaners, and when it came back I put it on with a white blouse early the next morning and went up to the reservoir. But it had been boarded over, and there was a chain-link fence around it. There was no way a girl of any size could get through."

You see, in Miss West's day, folks didn't give children shotguns as gifts.

The National Rifle Association insists that guns don't kill people. They do, nevertheless.

The 11-year-old Spartanburg boy had called an ambulance before he shot himself, which causes me to doubt that he really wanted to die.

After all, only three days earlier he had written a poem celebrating life:

Summer is a time of joys,
A time when laughter comes from girls and boys.
You run and jump and swim and play,
And that's what happens on a Summer day.

When I passed back through the park, one of the excited lads held up a crayfish, its tentacles waving wildly.

"You hafta know how to hold 'em!" he explained proudly.

The "firearms" lay ignored on the little bridge nearby.

Two wee lads, age 6, were doing what Jimmy might have done on a summer day— were it not for a handy gun. And an unhappy love affair.

At age 11.

July 1991

A wench in good condition

A few weeks ago, I wrote a column in which I quoted a friend of mine as saying he could not shoot a deer "laying down."

"Tell me," a critic said, "Why you let him get away with "laying" instead of "lying?"

"Because, he was a deer hunter, not a college professor, and his use of the word was perfectly natural. I have no quarrel with him. My quarrel is with the sports announcers, congressmen and college Ph.D.'s who go around fouling up the English language."

Over the holidays, a young house guest came into our home telling her dog to "Lay down!" On the day she departed, Shasta was "lying down."

Such grammatically correct miracles do not happen automatically. Somebody has to care about the language.

One of those who cares is Marvin Thompson, of Raleigh, who wrote recently and enclosed a classified ad that offered for sale a 1968 Bronco, "camaflaged with lift kit and wench in good condition."

"On the other hand," says Mr. Thompson, "this Bronco could come up with a serving wench who would bring you a cold beer after a long day's hunt."

Only last month, I heard a U.S. congressman and a Rhodes Scholar deliver a brilliant talk in Chapel Hill. But, silly as it seems, my high regard for him dropped a bit as he told about the woman who visited the Washington Zoo and saw a lion and a lamb "laying down together" in the same cage.

The woman, he said, went to the zoo manager and said, "Now I have seen everything! A lamb and a lion laying down together!" and the zoo manager explained, "Oh, that's not so unusual. We have to put in a new lamb every day."

Should I write the congressman and set him straight on the use of the verb? Would he appreciate it? After all, Gov. Bill Clinton is in a lot of trouble over "lie" and "lay."

Just this week, a researcher at McGill University in Canada announced that a single gene controls one's ability to learn grammar. Those lacking the gene, she said, are totally "worn out by just talking."

Hogwash! Another excuse for not learning and caring about grammar. When it comes to language, there are too many Rhett Butlers muttering, "Frankly my dear, I don't give a damn!"

An old newspaperman by the name of Normand Porrier once told a cub reporter that "The only thing that separates a lover from a liver is a vowel. Or a writer from a waiter, for that matter."

Or, in my opinion, an educated man from an uneducated one.

When told by a prelate that he had made a grammatical error in his opening address, Emperor Sigismund, in the year 1414, retorted, "I am King of the Romans and above grammar."

When it comes to grammar, our colleges are turning out thousands of Caesars who are "above grammar."

February 1992

What men want from life

The cover of the Newsweek I pulled out of the mailbox asked in a startling black headline: What do men really want?

Since it was high noon, my immediate want was a BLT, some Bing cherries, a salad and a cone of Zack's French vanilla yogurt.

Then I realized that Newsweek was asking a more serious, significant, encompassing question. What do men really want from life? And, subtly, from women?

First, let me say that the man on the Newsweek cover was definitely not me. He wore jeans, no shirt, a dark-striped, somewhat garish tie draped against a hairy chest.

In the crook of his right arm he carried a naked baby, under the other a goatskin tom-tom.

The next morning I conducted a short, quick "man-on-the-street" poll, asking several males, "What do men really want?"

The first three men replied, matter of factly, if not angrily: "I want to be left alone."

"Especially by my wife," one added.

Another said he wanted "more."

"More what?"

"More of everything," he said. "That's what men really want."

Asked what men want, one fellow said, "I'm not sure. But women are wrong in assuming that all men want is sex. Their wants go much deeper than that."

One well-married man replied, "I can't speak for every man. But what I want is the right not to divide the liriope. My wife keeps nagging me, and I'm just not gonna thin out all that liriope!"

"I want my back scratched," sighed one man. "Lots of men want that. But do they ever get it? No."

I know what he means. When my kids were small, I bribed them to scratch my back. But back-scratching now seems passe.

Just for the heck of it, I asked an attractive cashier at a downtown restaurant what men wanted.

"That's easy," she said. "They want three squares on the table every day, their socks matched and their underwear ironed."

"Ironed underwear! You must be kidding," I said. "Who wears ironed underwear? Real men don't wear ironed underwear."

The Newsweek article described how more and more men, in search of their wants, are attending all-male retreats, including "sweat lodges."

Jim Conn, a Methodist minister, recalling one "sweat lodge" experience said, "There was a lot of crying, screaming, yelling, gurgling sounds that came up."

Men do this, the article explained, because love and women are unable to heal the wounds of a man's childhood. The healing can come only from other men.

All in all, the article did not answer the magazine's own question: "What do men really want?" I suspect that every man wants a different thing on a different day.

But if I had to sum it up, I'd say that men want the same thing that women want: to be captain of their soul, with as little outside interference as possible.

But I like and agree with Newsweek's conclusion:

"Listen, hear that drumming? Is that the call of the tom-tom in the woods? Or the thump of your lonely heart?"

I doubt that sweating and yelling and beating drums with other men will provide a lasting, satisfying answer to man's searching. Or to his loneliness.

But it may ease the pain of disappointment and help him through another day, through such tasks as thinning liriope.

But I'm not for the sweating. Or the gurgling. The scars of my childhood will heal without that. In fact, the last time I looked, I didn't have any childhood scars.

What men want out of life changes year by year until, to many, it boils down to wanting a swift and painless exit.

July 1991

When boyfriends won't sleep over

A couple of weeks ago, a fellow called and asked if I would come out and speak to his singles club.

Unfortunately — or perhaps, fortunately — I had a conflict.

"We'd like for you to contrast dating with the way it was when you were single and the way it is today," the young man had said.

After I hung up the phone, I realized that I feel totally inadequate for the task. I could handle how courting went in my day. But the generation gap between my dating and today's presents a mind-boggling gulf.

As I walked through the newsroom on the way to a cup of coffee, a brightly colored book lying on a desk caught my attention.

Apparently it had strayed from the great stacks of volumes to be reviewed in the book editor's office nearby. Perhaps the book would equip me to talk to the singles club after all.

"Searching for Courtship," is by Winnifred B. Cutler, Ph.D.

I quickly realized it is directed primarily toward women, advising them on how to get their men without losing their dignity.

Remember, I said dignity, not virginity, which, once held in high esteem, seems to be routinely surrendered these days.

I still can't see the need for a "how to" book for every occasion. When I was young, you courted, not from a book, but by instinct, common sense and pure luck. Yet the marriages lasted and the vast majority of them were free of the violence that seems to pervade so many of today's marriages.

One chapter deals with recognizing "the magnetic power of a positive attitude," and whether or not your date will come on to it.

A 30-ish looking reporter looking over my shoulder said, "I wasn't worried about whether she'd come on to my positive attitude or not. I was worrying about whether the heater would work or whether one of the naked tires would blow before I got her home."

I didn't even have that to worry about.

Out of college, I didn't own a car. I had to date girls who did. Even in the '50s, nobody, not even "nice girls," was content only to sit in the porch swing of the rooming house where I lived, counting cars or watching TV in the parlor.

As time and I progressed, I came into my first car, a third-hand jeep purchased from my buddy who was getting married and moving up to his bride's Crown Victoria.

Things got even better. Eventually, I splurged on my greatest extravagance in life, a limited edition, hardtop, Carolina blue convertible.

At the push of a button, 16 separate motors went to work, lifting the metal top, folding it into three sections and stuffing it neatly into the trunk, then closing the trunk lid. Putting the top up or down would stop traffic and attract a great many girls.

Talk about a positive attitude. I had it!

In such a mood I met my wife. I had gone with my buddy — the former jeep owner — to Greensboro to select a red coat for his wife's Christmas present.

At a ritzy women's store, we were shown several red coats. We worried about getting the correct size.

"Oh, no problem," said the eager saleswoman. "A young woman I know from the college (UNC-G) is here also buying a red coat. I'll ask her to step over and model this one for you."

After the girl had modeled and gone, the saleswoman, holding the red coat against her chest, gushed to my buddy, "Anyone would be thrilled to find this under her tree on Christmas morning."

Nodding toward the trim, pretty girl with green eyes and honey-brown hair at the other end of the room, I said, "I'd be thrilled to find that under my tree...any old morning!"

How about that for "positive attitude!" We were promptly introduced and I started courting her in my Carolina-blue convertible, which, she told me later, "seemed awfully pretentious."

"I wasn't impressed by the car. I was impressed by you," she said. I never quite believed her.

One of the verities that caught my eye in Cutler's book was the comment, "You, as a female, have something a man wants."

So what else is new? Eve knew that much in the Garden of Eden.

The author expresses at least one legitimate concern in which the woman asks herself, "What would he be like in the garden I design — where I nourish him and he nourishes me? How would he change...What would the relationship that derives from those changes be?"

The author is talking about the garden of life, not that little drought-stricken plot out back where you are trying to grow tomatoes and okra.

As I thumb through this book, I doubt I will finish it. I've just arrived at a chapter that discusses such sensitive and hurtful issues as what to do when the boyfriend refuses to sleep over after having sex.

"Although he may tell you that when left alone overnight his dog is incontinent and his geraniums wilt, in courtship your needs must come before his dog's and his geraniums'," the author says.

Enough is enough! Obviously I am in over my head.

September 1993

The heart's keen anguish

Not long ago, I rode with two other men from the newspaper through the flat Eastern North Carolina countryside to attend graveside services for the mother of one of my best friends.

Dave's mother had died the death we all would choose. No pain, no sad goodbyes. At 90, she had enjoyed her evening meal, chatted with her daughter and son-in-law, with whom she lived, and then gone to bed.

Sometime in the night, her spirit, soul or whatever it is that makes us what we are quietly slipped away.

Spring was all about as we turned off Interstate 95 and entered the tiny community of Falcon, a place I had heard of but had never visited.

The spring sun warmed our backs as we stood near the grave. A mockingbird perched in a nearby magnolia tree trilled one operatic aria after another, like an aspiring soprano making a desperate debut at Carnegie Hall. At times, she almost drowned out the quiet, reassuring words of the Rev. J. Doner Lee.

The minister told how Ruth Jones had been a Culbreth, the daughter of one of the area's most prominent citizens and the very man who had named the place.

He told how in 1900, Julius Ainslie Culbreth, then 23, was asked to suggest a name for the new U.S. Post Office there.

Mr. Culbreth glanced at a box of pens on the shelf of his father's store and said, "Call it Falcon."

Looking about the flat tableland of greening fields and far horizons, and fluffy clouds skittering across the periwinkle sky, I felt a strange sense of loneliness here. Yet an equally strong sense of peace. I am tied by heart to hills and more rugged terrain.

Nearby, under an ancient magnolia, a weathered monument marked the resting place of Mrs. Jones's grandparents, who died in the same week in 1924.

Dimly legible are these words: "The heart's keen anguish only those can tell who bid the dearest and best farewell."

Then as now, these words are an appropriate sentiment for any loved one, particularly a parent, especially a mother.

As we left the cemetery, I couldn't help thinking of another recent funeral I had attended only in spirit.

It was the service for columnist Lewis Grizzard, a man less than half the age of my friend's mother.

A wickedly witty writer, Grizzard was unusually talented. He was a man of great success and equally great humility. He was a man of many wives, so many that Atlantans sported bumper stickers reading "Honk if you've never been married to Lewis Grizzard."

Lewis had written much, suffered much. He had a bad heart and was undergoing a second operation to transplant a heart valve from a pig when he died.

It's too bad that people can't read their obits before they die. Or perhaps it's just as well.

A Lyndon Johnson story has to do with a fellow reputed to be the meanest man in his community.

At his funeral, the preacher offered the floor to anyone who wanted to say something good about the deceased. No response. He pleaded again. And again. Finally, a man at the back of the church stood up.

"Speak out, Zeke," said the relieved preacher.

"His brother was worse," the fellow said, and sat down.

Lewis would have loved what his friend Furman Bisher of the Atlanta Journal-Constitution wrote after attending the funeral in Moreland, Ga.

According to Bisher, Lewis had wanted two songs sung at his funeral: "Amazing Grace" and "Precious Memories."

Bisher mentioned that at his own final rites, he wants someone to sing "How Great Thou Art."

What a coincidence. That's my only request. Perhaps that song has something to do with newspapering. Most writers are too cynical to publicly acknowledge the all-powerful Presence that most of us nevertheless feel at one time or another .

Furman Bisher made a point that I think of whenever I leave any funeral:

"The sun set on Moreland Tuesday, as it usually does. It arose again in the morning, as it usually does. That is to say that life goes on.

"But there is a hollowness in it, not that we shouldn't have come to reason by this time that in the end there is but one winner." Shakespeare wrote it the way it is best said, I guess:

Of all the wonders that I yet have heard,
It seems to me most strange that men should fear,
Seeing that death, a necessary end,
Will come when it will come.

Ah, yes, Mr. Shakespeare. But when we go and how we go make all the difference.

July 1994

Quarterbacks cry when hit

When Keith Fogleman called to invite me to accompany him to Chapel Hill for the Heels' set-to with Maryland, I cheerfully accepted. It was a day made for football!

And I had not been to Kenan in a couple of years, usually preferring to watch the televised games from a prone position on the den couch. Or better still, visiting the foothills apple orchards on a golden autumn afternoon.

On Saturday morning I slipped into a fresh pair of well-pressed khakis, put on a button-down shirt with a nifty tie, all topped off with a lightweight navy blazer.

When I rendezvoused with Keith and his friends at Fat Daddy's, I realized I had dressed for the wrong era.

"If you want to go home and change, we can wait," said Keith kindly, sensing my discomfort. Instead, I shucked off the tie and coat and unbuttoned the button-down.

Looking around the stadium, I spotted only one guy trussed up in coat and tie. Almost everyone, including many women, wore jeans and sports clothes. We have come a long way since women celebrated Saturday by wearing high heels, fur coats and their best dresses to football games, saving second best for church.

I mentioned the new stadium fashions to a friend, who said, "Oh yes, times have changed. I once had a roommate who said all she wanted out of life was a diamond ring, a fur coat and a chance to wear both to a football game in Kenan Stadium."

Gazing over the stadium on this gorgeous afternoon, I remembered how fellow student Andy Griffith, in town for a tent meeting, accidentally wandered into Kenan for his first glimpse of football.

"What It Was Was Football" launched the Tar Heel's spectacular career:

"I don't know, friend, to this day what it was that they were a-doin' down there, but I have studied about it," Andy said. "I think that it's some kind of a contest where they see which bunchful of them men can take that pumpkin and run from one end of that cow pasture to the other without either gettin' knocked down or steppin' in somethin'."

Keith is a more astute fan than I. He watches the linemen a lot and can pick up the holding violations even before the PA announcer spots them. I tend to keep my eyes on the quarterback, the game's control center.

You don't have to be a sports fan to enjoy George Plimpton's book "Paper Lion." Plimpton, a writer, in 1966 had the courage and lack of good sense to spend five weeks in preseason scrimmage with the Detroit Lions. As the quarterback, he actually ran a series of plays in an exhibition game before a full stadium.

He describes the great sense of power that every quarterback — from midget football to Super Bowl champs — must feel on the field.

"Everything fine about a quarterback — the embodiment of his power — was encompassed in those dozen seconds or so: giving the instructions to 10 attentive men, breaking out of the huddle, walking for the line, and then pausing behind the center, dawdling amidst men poised and waiting under the trigger of his voice, cataleptic, until the deliverance of himself and them to the future."

Plimpton's four plays are disastrous, moving the team backward 29 yards, only a yard away from a safety.

On the verge of tears, he discusses his miserable performance later with philosophical coach George Wilson. He can't understand why he cries when he's hit.

"I have these tear ducts which react quickly to being hit....I suspect it embarrasses my opponents — to see that tear-streaked puss opposite them."

Coach Wilson reassures him:

"When kids, out in the park, choose up sides for tackle rather than touch, the guys that want to be ends and go out for passes, or even quarterback, because they think subconsciously they can get rid of the ball before being hit, those guys don't end up as football players.

"They become great tennis players or skiers, or high jumpers. It doesn't mean they lack courage or competitiveness. But guys who put up their hands to be tackles and guards or fullbacks who run not for daylight but for trouble — those are the ones who one day will make it as football players."

In the future, I am going to follow Keith's example and spend more time watching the line where the courage runs deeper and men don't cry.

Organized sports — college as well as professional — frequently come under criticism, much of it justified. But tell me, is there a better classroom where the lessons of life are taught more dramatically and effectively than here?

Like the Romans of old, unfortunately, many fans enjoy the violence and the final score more than they appreciate the skill, the timing and endurance the game commands.

It's the latter that I take off my tie to!

September 1993

Ode to a 'first violinist'

Petite, maybe 5 feet, 2 inches tall, she taught me Latin in the eighth grade.

Many a country lad and city kid who thought they could push her around soon learned that not only is all Gaul divided into three parts, but also that Miss Beatrice Holbrook had it all together. She brooked no foolishness from anybody.

Last week, Grady Cooper and I drove four hours through the fog and rain to the village of Traphill in Wilkes County to say a final farewell to this remarkable woman.

I remember her for many things — her zest for life, her dedication to teaching and to preserving the history of her foothills county. I remember her also because twice in the same class period, she banished Grady and me.

We were anything but hell raisers by today's student standards. And it really wasn't our fault.

It was just that during an inopportune moment, Eunice Ann Mastattler, a country girl who had ripened early in a sensual way, confided to the boys at our table that she was so passionate, "hot" was her word, that she had to "pee in the creek to keep from setting the woods on fire."

Caught by surprise by this quaint expression, we freaked out. You know how it is when, sometimes even in church, you think you'll explode if you can't let go and guffaw.

Miss Holbrook, her face frozen in icy disapproval, excused the two of us "until you can behave like gentlemen."

Readmitted to the classroom 10 minutes later, we were OK until Eunice Ann threw us a wicked wink. We were off — and out — again.

At the end of the month, for the first time in my life, I took home a "C" on conduct.

My mother was furious. She could forgive an F in Latin but never a C in conduct. But how could I tell her about Eunice Ann's fear of setting the woods on fire?

During a recent dinner party, a guest remarked that she would be going home that same night, a Sunday, to tackle a stack of 300 eighth-grade compositions and spelling tests.

She was, of course, an English teacher, one of those afflicted with the curse of commitment.

You've met a few of these academic workhorses who make a difference in kids' lives, teaching them how to write a decent sentence, introducing them to William Faulkner, Emily Dickinson and Ernest

Hemingway.

These teachers don't spend much time in the teachers' lounge. Another guest aptly described them as "the violinists in the symphony?"

"How's that?" I asked.

"Haven't you observed the guys with the cymbals and the triangle? Why they could sit back and read 'War and Peace' during Beethoven's Fifth. Or walk down to Greenshields for a beer during Mozart's 'Eine Kleine Nachtsmusik,' just as long as they're back in time to tap that little triangle or smash those cymbals together.

"But not the violinists. They're always there, patiently sawing away," he added.

Yes, I have noticed. I've also wondered if the percussion people get paid the same as the sweating violinists in the way our state pays the teacher who never takes papers home the same it does one who wrestles with 300 each week.

Curious, I called up my friends at the North Carolina Symphony. Hold your hat! They do get the same thing, except for the concertmaster and the first violinist. I'm sure there's a good reason, though I can't think of one.

In a tiny, white church nestled against the foot of the mountain, we sang "The Battle Hymn of the Republic" and other hymns. We heard moving testimonials from people who knew, admired and loved Miss B.

In this way we said goodbye to her — first violinist in that small symphony of teachers whose music we remember.

February 1991

Losing virginity worth a page

When I go out to the schools to talk to students about writing, I encourage them to keep journals in which they confide their innermost thoughts, their hurts, passions and secret longings.

Writing, I tell them, is a kind of therapy. It may save the cost of a shrink further along in life. I also encourage them to write letters — to anyone.

I once kept a diary, in the eighth grade. I came across it a few years ago and trashed it. Written in code, most of it was unintelligible.

With some effort, I figured some of it out. "PGLCELM," for example, meant "Please God, let Carmen Edwards like me."

In a shy kid with acne, it was a heartfelt plea.

In a 1983 volume of columns, Chicago Tribune writer Bob Greene included one about a diary he kept the summer he was 17.

Keeping diaries has something to do with sensitive people who write. Plumbers and CPAs never kept diaries as kids.

Bob's diary, at 17, was a lot more exciting than mine at 14.

In a June 1964 entry, he describes how a buddy made love for the first time, unaware that his friends were listening.

"Locked ourselves in bathroom — they came in — started to talk — quiet for 20 minutes — then he said, 'I can't get the damn package open' — but he did and he got her good —— she was breathing real hard and crying a lot."

Like all boys of that age, Bob felt the peer pressure to lose his virginity:

"It sounded like hell," he said, referring to his friend's sexual experience, "but it's just something I have to do. That's my goal for this summer."

Some people also save letters. I now wish I had.

My wife remembers a couple of high school classmates whose stormy romance revolved around their letters.

"They'd have a fight and Harvey would go over to Laverne's house and demand his love letters. She'd hand them over, tied up in a pink ribbon. Then they'd make up and Harvey would return the letters.

"This happened three or four times. But one day when Harvey again demanded his letters, Laverne yelled 'Harvey, I have burned those damned letters.' That time, they broke up for good."

Speaking of letters, Dr. Wells Edmundson of Raleigh recently came across a classic while going through the personal effects of his late grandfather, a Baptist minister.

Apparently, it had been brought to the minister by a woman parishioner who clearly was in desperate need of consolation. I have never read a more devastating letter.

"Miss Celia," it began. "The great love I have hitherto expressed for you is false...The more I see of you, the more you appear in my eyes an object of contempt....Believe me, I never had any intention to offer you my hand. Our last conversation has left a tedious insipidity, which has by no means given me the most exalted idea of your disposition.

"Your temper would make me extremely unhappy; and if we were united, I shall experience nothing but the hatred of my parents, added to everlasting displeasure in living with you.

"...If you will do me a favor to avoid me, I shall excuse you taking the trouble to answer this. Your letters are always full of impertinence, and you have not a shadow of wit and good sense. Adieu.' Harold Sears."

Since today's young people don't write letters, what do they take back when they break up? Their sweaters or sweat-shirts? Beach towels they have shared?. The mudflaps on their cars?

And, from what I hear, losing one's innocence is not nearly the big deal it once was.

I called Bob Greene in Chicago to see if he kept his vow to score in the summer of '64.

"No, not that summer," he chuckled. "It was some time later."

March 1991

Sin, serendipity in the foothills

I am back from the foothills, happy to report that in the mountains, the trees hang heavy with apples, the Goldens being picked daily, the Winesaps due around the first of October.

My niece and her husband, who joined us for breakfast at the Hungry Farmer, were full of curiosity about an abandoned car they had seen at a Blue Ridge Parkway overlook on the way over to Surry.

The car, minus license tag, was locked. A pair of panties and a bra lay on the back seat. On the driver's seat was an airline ticket; on the passenger side, a white Bible.

From such a find, a fellow with an ounce of imagination could concoct a touching short story or an absorbing mystery thriller.

They are still fighting sin in the foothills.

A local minister had seen a woman pull into a grocery store parking lot at dusk, jump out, lock her car and get into a waiting car with a man. She lay down on the back seat as the car sped away.

The preacher left a note on the windshield: "Be sure, your sins will find you out."

They've added a new stoplight to my hometown and have done away with angle parking. As my sister drives two blocks past the courthouse, looking for a straight-in place to park, I am thinking, "Women's lib, where are you when they really need you?"

Up in apple country, I learned that Omah Boyd's husband, who was called up during Operation Desert Storm, is still in uniform, although he needs to be home mowing the orchard and harvesting apples.

We were welcome to pick our own, she said. But the orchard is so overgrown with weeds there is a risk of snakes, she warns.

Allergic to serpents, I drove on down to visit Mabel Utt, whose trees also are laden this year.

But the honey crop is way short.

"The bees produced only about half a crop," Mrs. Utt sighs, gesturing toward half a dozen jars of golden sweetness.

"Yeah, bees are just like people, getting lazier every day," I suggested.

"Oh, no, it was not the bees' fault. It was the lack of blossoms. There are no lazy bees," she said loyally.

I dropped in on a couple who have been married for more than 50 years. They were wed when she was a very pretty, mere slip of a girl of 16 years.

"Ah, yes, I remember taking her flowers," he said, recalling their courtship.

"Wildflowers," she explained, just for the record.

"I'll bet you never even had another boyfriend," I suggested.

"Oh yes I did. I had two before him. They're both dead. I suppose I should have married one of them," she mused, her eyes full of mischief.

I rode with my sister to Fairview Baptist Church for a covered-dish supper and to meet her new minister, the Rev. Mark Phillips. Just out of the seminary, he is settling into his first pastorate.

He is a young, likable fellow, who is introducing some refreshing ideas to a rather staid, traditional congregation.

And, like most new ministers, he is being showered with attention — and food — by the ladies of the church.

There is a mystique about ministers that almost compels affection, if not adoration. And yet, in the latest Gallup Poll on most-trusted professions, pharmacists nosed out preachers as the most trustworthy.

Yes, used-car salesmen again finished last.

Outside the little church, I stood alone in the gathering twilight, gazing across the green expanse of fields of corn and tobacco toward Pilot Knob, rising purple in the distance.

The stillness was broken only by the sleepy sighing of insects in the grass and the whirring of locusts in the big oaks, shrilly sounding the swan song of summer.

I am no Bible scholar. But as I stood there soaking up the serenity, a line came to me from somewhere deep in the Scriptures: "Be still and know that I am God."

September, 1991

A hero without magic

What I am saying to you today has been on my mind for some time.

Ever since a member of my wife's book club, confused by the presession chatter about the Magic Johnson affair, whispered to one of the members, "Who is Magic Johnson?"

No, this wasn't Rip Van Winkle waking from a long century's nap. There were a few people who hadn't heard of Magic Johnson before his AIDS announcement.

None are that ignorant now. Magic Johnson is the new national hero. And that bothers me a bit.

I share some of the feeling of Slats Grobnick, syndicated columnist Mike Royko's fictional sidekick.

"I thought to be a hero you had to do something brave and not selfish and something that would help other people. When you cut through all the media hype, besides being a great basketball player, what did he do?

"He was out there hopping in the sack with one bimbo after another. That's how he picked up the virus, right?"

And old Slats went on to describe how in service, the chaplains and the medics went to great lengths to warn us against unsafe sex. Ah, many of you ex-soldiers remember.

"They'd have a picture show with what your whoozits would look like if you wasn't careful." Slats said.

And he recalled that when some of his buddies became infected, they'd have to report to the first sergeant.

"And I never heard of any first sergeant saying, 'Glad you're taking it so well, private, you're a hero.' He usually said you were a bozo and would give you an extra week of KP for goofing up."

Now you may say that Slats Grobnick and Mike Royko are being entirely too harsh. This is not gonorrhea, we're talking about, you say. This is a deadly disease.

You're right about the latter. And we're right to feel sympathy for Magic Johnson, who from what I can tell, is one really sweet guy, a prince in a profession that includes its fair share of scoundrels and a great deal of arrogance.

But when I think of heroes, I don't think of people who are careless in choosing their sexual partners, even if they do beat the media to the punch by calling their own news conference.

In a recent magnificent, two-hour Academy Awards type spectacular,

Walt Disney Inc. introduced us to 36 of America's best public school teachers. Filmed sketches of these teachers utilizing their skills, talent and dedication made my hair stand on end.

Now that's what I call magic. But too often our teachers' magic is wasted on indifferent and unappreciative parents and the public.

If one of our great teachers came down with AIDS, would we rally behind him or her? More than likely, we'd be wanting the teacher out of the classroom.

Every day, we hear about friends or relatives who, through no fault of their own, are stricken by a terminal disease.

Many are salt-of-the-earth types who have spent years quietly ministering to families, friends and their communities.

But nobody honors them as heroes, although their personal courage in facing death tears at our very hearts.

Slats Grobnick asked about the women that Magic Johnson may have infected. Perhaps they, too, should be honored as heroines.

"Why not?" he said. "They were just doing the old two-to-tango like he was. And maybe with the same results. Maybe they could become role models for other young ladies who ain't too bright or careful, like Magic is gonna do for guys who ain't too bright or careful."

Now that Slats and I have said all this, I will keep on feeling sorry for Magic Johnson, a nice guy who is very sick.

I also will continue feeling sorry that we live in a time so short on heroes that we have come to this.

That, too, is a national sickness.

November 1991

There's joy in feeling guilty

Hey, how's your guilt level? Is it keeping you awake at night or preventing you from having a good time when you've worked hard and earned a good time?

Does your conscience nag you about the time you snapped at the kids as they were heading off to school? Or for something you didn't do for your favorite aunt before she passed on?

I once heard a man say, in the presence of his wife, that he never has trouble falling asleep at night.

"That's because I have a clear conscience," he explained.

"That's not because you have a clear conscience. That's because you have a poor memory!" his wife retorted.

Well, you can unload your guilt on a psychiatrist's couch. Or leave it with your pastor or priest. Or, as a last resort, you can take it to "Mr. Apology." More about that later.

Although I've been a Protestant all my life, I like the Catholics' arrangement whereby they go to confession, tell all and get relief from a guilty conscience.

A Catholic friend told me an amusing story about a young fellow of 16 or so who went to confession and admitted he had sassed his mom, stolen from his brother and, for the first time, gone all the way with a girl.

The priest pressed him for the name of the girl, to which he replied, "Oh no, Father! I couldn't!

"Was it Katie O'Shaunessey?" the clergyman asked.

"No," said the boy.

"Was it Mary Margaret Murphy?"

The answer was still no.

"Was it Colleen McClinty?

The boy sighed and said nothing. The priest ordered him to do so many Stations of the Cross, say a hundred Hail Marys and skip meat for a week.

Upon leaving the confessional, the boy was met by two of his buddies who wanted to know how things went.

"The bad news is I gotta do a lot of prayers," he said. "But the good news is I have the names of two other girls!"

I had never heard of "Mr. Apology," America's call-in confessional, until I read about him in an issue of The Guardian I picked up in a London train station.

According to the article, "Mr. Apology" is the pseudonym for the New York City artist and former carpenter and shoplifter who founded the popular nonprofit telephone service in 1980.

"Mr. Apology" receives an average of 100 calls daily on his complex, computerized voice mail. Some call to listen to other people's confessions. Others confess to offenses ranging from spitting on hamburgers served to police officers to actual murder.

"I'd like to apologize to my boyfriend, Harold," one woman said. "We've been together for 11 years and I've been cheating on him for eight."

"Sometimes when I'm in a really good mood," said another caller, "I dance on the table naked and then I eat mangoes and then I go get the mail."

Lisa called to apologize to her dead grandmother for not crying enough at her funeral.

"I never actually, you know, heaved," she said.

A painter and a decorator addressed his apology to all those clients whose wives he had slept with while on the job.

Guardian reporter Jonathan Freedland makes a good point. The Apology Line, he says, is an outgrowth of the current American fetish for self-revelation, the kind of stuff you see on the Oprah Winfrey and Phil Donahue shows.

Mr. Apology gets a vicarious thrill out of listening to others tell of their wickedness.

"I recognize aspects of evil in myself," he says, admitting, however, that he would make a lousy priest or therapist.

Some people avoid guilt like the plague. Others wallow in guilt.

Susan Stamberg, in her "Every Night at Five" book, quotes a New Yorker obsessed with guilt:

"I feel guilty about not getting to work on time. I feel guilty about getting to work too early. I feel guilty about getting to work on time and making other people feel that they should have gotten to work at the same time.

"I feel guilty about getting up too early in the morning because I might wake somebody up. I feel guilty about sleeping too late because they might have to creep around and not disturb me, and I don't want them to feel bad.

"You see what I mean. Once you're into it, the whole world opens up for you."

As I see it, the way to handle guilt is to pass it around, assuming only your rightful share and being truly sorry for your portion.

August 1994

Lacking the killer instinct

The man who said it doesn't matter who won or lost, but how you played the game never played Scrabble with an 18-year-old with an SAT score of 1,540 and a burning passion to win.

It happened during the holidays. After a feast at my sister-in-law Susan's house, someone suggested we play Scrabble.

I hadn't played for years, but certainly felt up to beating an average or better player. And certainly an 18-year-old.

The contest, I learned, was to be primarily between me and the young man, also a house guest. We squared off at the dining room table, Craig with his father as his second, and I, with my wife as mine.

My first seven tiles were good ones. On one play alone, I scored 58 points. It was then that I looked across the table and observed my opponent's hand clenching and unclenching and the steely glint in his young, clear eyes.

"What have we here?" I thought.

In the Sports Department, where I occasionally write, I came across "Winning is an Attitude," by John Chaney, coach of the Temple Owls. It seems that every sports figure — player, coach, fan — has a book in him.

In one of the blurbs on the dust cover, Coach Chaney says, "If you go into any kind of contest overly emotional, it's almost like being drunk. It's like drinking a bottle of whiskey before the game.

"In any aspect of life, you just can't be emotionally drunk. Emotion only stays with you a short period. What you want is a sustained effort of performance. Not just on the basketball court, but throughout life."

I certainly didn't go into the Scrabble game "overly-emotional." But it didn't take long for me to realize I was engaged in a very serious, no-holds-barred contest.

My young opponent was not outwardly emotional as he considered every word possibility, working them out on paper as Einstein might have labored over the theory of relativity. He privately consulted his father from time to time.

Impatient with the long time between plays, my wife abandoned me to chat with her sister. I was relieved, since she had kept urging me to "go ahead and play."

"No way!" I snapped. "I want to win, too!"

"This is getting too serious for me," she said. "It's only a word game."

My luck held. I kept drawing the big-point tiles. Still, the kid kept coming, like John McEnroe, down but never out, skillfully racking up good scores with his measly one-pointer "i's" and "o's" and an occasional four-point "h" or "y."

Meanwhile, my two daughters and my young nephews stood behind me, urging me on.

Suddenly, I realized the game had developed into an "us" against "them" situation that I did not like. Still, I felt the pressure to uphold my family's honor.

An hour and a half later, Craig had beaten me by 15 points or so. And as I walked away from the table, he was still looking for a place to play his last tile, a one-point "e" as the coup de grace for an already defeated enemy.

Even in a Scrabble game, we learn about ourselves. I now realize that I have never been as competitive as I might have been, that I have never had the killer instinct, except in rare instances.

I am not a "dunker." And I have too much compassion for my opponents. I always want to salvage their self-respect in defeat.

Subconsciously I suppose I have shared the philosophy of Elwood P. Dowd, the hero of the play "Harvey" by Mary Chase:

"When I was a boy, my mother said to me, 'Elwood, in this world you have to be ever so smart or ever so pleasant.' For years I tried smart. I recommend pleasant."

A nice thought. Still, we need to keep in mind that this was a guy who was in and out of mental institutions and talked to a big white rabbit that did not exist.

February 1991

Tell the girl in Tony's room

He had gone back to the out-of-state university to pick up after his son. A footlocker left behind, along with a small refrigerator. And the "Fuzz Buster" the boy had loaned to a friend.

He knocked on the door of the dorm room, where the boy's roommate had promised to meet him. No answer. He knocked again, harder. The door swung open as if moved by some mysterious hand.

A form lay under the blanket on the bottom bunk.

"Hey, Tony!" he shouted. "Wake up, Tony!"

The form stirred, kicked off the blanket, revealing a young woman, her miniskirt up to her navel. Her pantyhose was torn at the knee and at other places. She snored loudly, with her mouth open.

"Where's Tony?" the man yelled.

"Tony ain't here?" muttered the zonked-out coed, resuming her snoring.

The intruder backed out of the room, marveling as he went at the accumulation of dirt, the pile of dirty underwear and bed sheets, the strewn books and papers and the 200 or so crushed beer cans.

He was amazed that humans could live under conditions that swine would find intolerable.

Driving north up the straight, clean highway in the darkness toward home, he inwardly wept for the way it once was, for that good time when going to college was better than it is now, when there was moonlight on the magnolias, and you studied Hemingway and Wolfe, and had to have your date back to the dorm by midnight.

"I know the world is not what it used to be," said my friend, a realist. "But even so, do they have to get right down in the gutters of life? Is there no point at which they say, 'This is as far as I go?'"

"I think so. For some," I said optimistically.

It's not easy to pinpoint the exact time when purity became passe and cleanliness was no longer even close to godliness.

Many of us like to point the finger at our colleges and universities, which, in effect, said in the '60s, "Send us your sons and daughters, your beloved, your future hopes, and we will let them drink long and deep from the fount of knowledge.

"But we will no longer tuck them in at night or tell them to write home once a month. Or really care if they use their dorms for brothels. We are not your children's keepers."

I can better understand that attitude today. For by the time our colleges get our children, they have been exposed to just about every experience possible. Many of them, when they check into their freshman dorm, are barely literate in the academics. But many are Phi Beta Kappa in such subjects as sex, drugs and alcohol.

It might have helped if, back in the '60s, college officials had stood firm by such standards as "in by midnight" and "no men or liquor on the halls."

Instead, they established "anything goes" dorms, arranged campus beer blasts on the quad and began dispensing condoms at the Student Union.

Not long ago, a recreation major in my wife's public speaking class at N.C. State shocked her fellow-students.

"The trouble with students today is that they don't know how to use their lesiure time,' she said.

"Instead of spending it doing drugs, having sex and getting drunk every night, you ought to be visiting our national parks. It's a lot cheaper. And safer."

If I had written such a thing in a column, my young readers would have scoffed. Or laughed out loud. But with such advice coming from one of their own, they might think about it.

At least they know by now they won't get AIDS by snuggling up to a loblolly pine at Umstead Park.

But before all under age 24 rush out to embrace our national forests, please, will somebody run by Tony's room, wake the girl in the torn pantyhose and give her the good news?

January 1992

It's never 'only a game'

Realizing that tension—like lasagna, pecan pie and other good stuff—is not good for my health, I had avoided State-Carolina football for several years.

The realization that I should have stayed home Saturday first hit me during the singing of the national anthem, when a woman behind me kept screaming at somebody, "Take your hat off, you pig!"

The next ominous omen appeared as a covey of crows flew over the stadium in formation, undoubtedly arranged for by Agriculture Commissioner Jim Graham to remind old grads that the university once was known as Cow College.

Ron Butler, head guru for NCSU's Friends of the College, came from across the aisle to ask who I was going to pull for.

"I'm on whoever side God's on," I said tartly, knowing full well that God doesn't suit up for football or any other sport, no matter what people say.

Then, turning to my wife, he said, "Oh, Nancy, I have a letter in the mail to you. You won two tickets to Friends of the College this year."

I groaned inwardly. That's the kind of luck we have at our house.

We never win the Reader's Digest Sweepstakes or the Virginia state lottery.

I've won two things in my whole life: an electric shoe polisher at the office Christmas party in 1973, and, while a cub reporter in Burlington, an oil and lube at a time when I didn't own a car.

FOC is a fabulous concert series. But when you have been going for 26 seasons, there comes a time when you say, "I am not going back to hear Burl Ives sing 'Blue Tail Fly' one more time."

Especially when you sit so far from the stage that big ol' Burl looks like a fly-speck on a piece of white construction paper.

Sidney and Rachel Eagles sat right behind us at the ballgame.

When State scored, Sid, a judge on the state Court of Appeals, imparted some of the judicial wisdom that got him where he is today.

"Just remember," he said, "that when your team wins, it's a great victory. But when your team loses, it's just another game."

State scored again. Bedlam broke out! I looked around to find my own wife jumping up and down like a high school cheerleader. I gave her Wolfpack red skirt a yank and thought, "This is what women's lib has brought us to."

Here came Butler again.

"Oh, you've come to take the Friends of College tickets back," I said hopefully.

"No, I've come to see if you know by now whose side God is on," he crowed.

The judge tapped me on the shoulder. "Remember, for you, it's only a game."

I kept wondering why the Carolina coach didn't put in that fantastic quarterback for whom he moved heaven and earth to get academically qualified.

Then I remembered that one of the men in the Sports Department had explained that to me. It's a matter of protocol.

"You just don't do that," he said. "You don't humiliate the regular guy in front of his relatives and girlfriend, even if it means losing the game. How would you have felt if, in your prime, the editor had replaced you on the statehouse beat with a young, hotshot J-school grad and assigned you to covering seed spitting contests at the Farmer's Market?"

We had to leave in the third quarter to visit my mother-in-law in High Point. I never dreamed that visiting one's mother-in-law could be an exciting alternative to watching the Heels play on a golden autumn afternoon.

The Wolfpack administered the coup de grace as I rode toward High Point. I won't say that my day was ruined. But it wasn't enhanced when, as we walked in the door, my mother-in-law said to my wife, "I watched the game on TV. I'm glad your team won."

Judge Eagles is wrong. It's never only a game.

October 1991

Velvet I would wish her

It's not as if she is leaving us for the first time. We have said goodbye before. When she went to camp in the summer or to Nantucket to wait on tables. Or to Blue Heaven for four years of college.

All of you who have raised and loved a daughter, or a son for that matter, know the tug at the heartstrings at each stage of the letting go season. But usually they've been only a telephone call and a checkbook away.

But when you give away your daughter to another man, it's quite another story. Quite another feeling.

This, my daughter's wedding day, was so swift in coming. Too swift, in fact.

It seems like such a short time ago that her first date rang the doorbell. I had donned a shirt and tie for the occasion. But there he stood, as frightened as a young buck, a gangly kid in tennis shoes with a lock of unruly hair. He introduced himself as Tom, or was it Steve? Or Kevin?

No, it wasn't Kevin. I would have remembered Kevin. Even before I married I planned to name my first son Kevin. Fortunately, God, in his wisdom, gave two delightful daughters to a man who has never bent a fishing pole and who, as a kid, always dropped the pop-up fly in left field.

I do remember that the boy's handshake was wet with perspiration. And I remember how, when they drove away in the dusk, my wife ran down the street after them, screaming, "Turn on your lights! Turn on your lights!" and wailing over and over "Oh, she's going to be killed!"

At the rehearsal dinner, the father is expected to make a toast. In November, on a trip to New York, we enjoyed Frank Loesser's wonderful Broadway musical, "Guys and Dolls."

In it, Sarah, the Salvation Army lass, confides to her grandfather that yes, much to her distress, she is in love with Sky Masterson, the gambler.

Whereupon the old man sings the words of advice that all dads might give to their daughters on their wedding day.

Velvet I can wish you
For the collar of your coat
And fortune smiling all along your way.
But more I cannot wish you
Than to wish you find your love
Your own true love this day.

Mansions I can wish you,
Seven footmen all in red,
And calling cards upon a silver tray.
But more I cannot wish you
Than to wish you find your love
Your own true love this day.

Katherine Victoria was born during a January blizzard. I can't recall a more apprehensive time, before or since.

As I sat in the waiting room with the other expectant fathers, most younger than I, a nurse walked in and said to one, "Congratulations! You have a fine little girl."

"Damn!" the man muttered, tossing aside a magazine. "I wanted a boy."

I wanted to hit the guy. Those who have wanted, waited and lost have a special appreciation for the miracle of birth. As well as for its miscues.

After what seemed a very long while, Dr. Robert Ruark, the fatherly obstetrician who had walked us through our disappointments came lumbering down the hall.

I searched his face for a sign. Please, no bad news this time.

"A.C.," he said, a grin creasing his rugged face, "You have a little girl who, unfortunately, looks a lot like you. But with the passage of time and God's help she may outgrow it."

I like Adam. I like him a lot. Kind, witty and also a journalist, he is all I could want in a son-in-law. But I keep thinking about a little story, supposedly true, told by a minister friend some years ago. Why is it that ministers and lawyers seem to know all the best stories?

A little girl, looking through a telescope for the first time, told her mother that she saw God.

"And what does God look like, dear?" the mother asked.

"He looks a lot like Daddy." the child answered simply.

I remember the time when in my daughter's eyes, mine was that face at the far end of the telescope. But it is my feeling now that, were she asked, she might well answer that He looks a lot like the young man she is marrying today.

That's the way it should be. I would not want it otherwise. Still, giving away a part of your heart is never easy.

May 1993

The melodies linger on

On the car radio, Rush Limbaugh arrives at the stroke of noon, forcing me to flee WPTF and such favorite personalities as Maury O'Dell and Donna Mason. So I quickly switch to WCPE, which deals with classical stuff. And when the violins become too shrill or the Beethoven too brooding, I jump over to Light Eight-Five.

Sometimes I linger longer than I should, listening to songs with real words, sweet harmony and pure nostalgia. I realized only recently how our lives, yours and mine, are measured by songs. The mind is a veritable picture album of sound.

"Blue Tango," takes me back to my bachelor days in Burlington, where I shared a flat with friend Joe Davidson. Joe had an irritating habit of coming in from a late date and putting on a stack of records and crawling into his bed.

"Blue Tango," was always the last to fall, and it would tango all night long unless I crawled out of bed and turned off the record player. "Blue Tango" will forever be associated with my old buddy from my bachelor days.

"My Happiness" was stamped indelibly on my brain when I was a senior in high school. Those of us who rode the second bus would congregate in the auditorium where the Dockery twins and Delia Long would, with a tear in their voices, harmonize: "Every day I reminisce, dreaming of your tender kiss, thinking only how I miss, my happiness."

Faraway places with strange-sounding names tore at the heart of a homesick kid 10,000 miles, a war and a world away from Surry County.

"Fly the ocean in a silver plane, see the jungle when it's wet with rain," the song would go.

World War II provided too many faraway places with strange-sounding names, such as Nadzab, Biak, Pelileu, Okinawa, Tachikawa, etc. I became weary of wet jungles and silver planes. "But remember all the while, darling, you belong to me" had little meaning for me then.

At Mars Hill Junior College, tucked in the hills beyond Asheville, I heard for the first time the haunting song "The Way You Look Tonight." It was a favorite of my impetuous friend and weekend roommate, Julian Hamrick, who hitchhiked every weekend from Chapel Hill to pay court to cute, petite Susie Betlem. Neither of them ever knew that I also had a crush on Susie.

The words I have forgotten, the melody lingers on. The song is "More," played over and over by the ship's orchestra during a week-long Bermuda cruise that my wife and I took in the early '60s B.C.

(Before Children.)

Amid attacks of seasickness, I stuffed six meals a day, danced far into the night and shopped the island boutiques when in port.

Every time I stumbled nauseated to the ship's rail or came close to collapsing on my feet from exhaustion, or pleaded to sleep in, my wife would say, "Oh, come on, honey! We may not pass this way again."

When I hear "ring out those lazy, hazy days of summer, a summer of soda, and pretzels and beer" I travel back to Blowing Rock's Farm House Restaurant and a roof-raising rendition by the singing waiters and waitresses.

I also remember how, next morning in our motel room, while the children played happily in a corner, Richard Nixon, on TV, wept bitterly as he surrendered his presidency.

"Come sit by my side little darlin...come lay your cool hand on my brow...promise me that you will never...be nobody's darlin' but mine."

That plaintive country tune takes me back to when I was 12 and looked upon the face of death for the first time.

A neighbor's strapping 19-year-old son — discovering that his darlin' was also somebody else's darlin' — went home and put a bullet through his heart.

We went by the farmhouse to pay our respects. And as I looked down on the handsome, waxen face, I shivered at the thought of my own mortality, and turned away with wonder and confusion. How could this thing called love cause someone so young to want to stop living?

"Sentimental Journey." The scene is a huge airplane hangar at Tachikawa Air Force Base, south of Tokyo, Japan. The war has ended. The orders for home have come. I'm finally taking that sentimental journey home.

Across the vast expanse of cots and duffel bags, GIs are packing up. I turn to shake the hand of Gorrell Westmoreland of Nacogdoches, Texas.

Two years together in the same tent leads to a lot of bonding. But it's goodbye ol' buddy time.

"We'll stay in touch," he says.

"Sure," I say. We know we won't. We never did.

Your life has its own musical score, perhaps similar, perhaps different from mine. I'm just grateful I don't have to rely on today's popular songs as custodians of my memories.

June 1993

Rare moments when men cry

A I saw in the paper that longtime friend and public servant Roy Tilley of Fuquay-Varina was "overcome by emotion" when he switched his party affiliation from Democrat to Republican.

Changing parties may be something to tear at a man's emotions. I don't know. Anyway, Roy let it be known he cried for joy.

I do know that men are not expected to show emotion in public. Men rarely cry. But we've all had our moments:

Holding your newborn in your arms for the first time. Scoring a touchdown in the championship game. Receiving an award before an audience of friends and fellow professionals. Winning the Spivey's Corner hollering contest.

Men coming home from war have cried openly at their first glimpse through the fog of the Statue of Liberty or the Golden Gate Bridge. Even tough old General "Dug-out Doug" MacArthur wept against his will during his "Old soldiers never die" swan song.

And as every kid who had to memorize Bible verses and went for the shortest one knows very well that even Jesus wept publicly.

But only twice. Once, upon learning of the death of Lazarus, and again over the impending destruction of Jerusalem.

Oh sure, some men weep at funerals. From boyhood, I remember relatives returning from the church saying that so and so "took it real hard."

In one case, a man I know was so overcome by grief that he had to be restrained from climbing into the casket with his beloved wife. Nine months later he had remarried.

But, for the most part, weeping openly is not the sort of thing society expects of men. When it does occur, it can be a traumatic experience.

It happened to me several years ago during a speech to the Wake County SPCA, a noble organization if there ever was one.

I had planned to take along Amazing Grace, our much-loved, 14-year-old black poodle that I had written about occasionally. I couldn't have had a better "show and tell" item for this particular audience.

I got along fine until, near the end of the speech, I tried to explain why the dog wasn't with me.

Suddenly, there flashed across my mind the scene at the vet's office three days earlier: my wife holding the little black, cancer-riddled fluff of fur in her arms, the dog's trusting eyes on her face as the doctor injected the needle that took her forever from her pain.

One night in late September my daughter, whose husband is a

reporter on the St. Petersburg Times, called to tell me of an unusual incident that occurred in the outlying town of Dunedin. Times writer Tom Zucco described the scene in the clipping she sent me later.

It was "helmet night" and the stands were full at Grant Field, the town's baseball park where the hometown Blue Jays and the Fort Lauderdale Red Sox were locked up in a close Class A game.

Dunedin pitcher Dennis Gray, a 23-year-old from Banning, Calif., had a one-hitter going after six innings, when suddenly from the side of the field, a little boy, mentally retarded, broke away from his mother and rushed out to the pitcher's mound.

The umpires called time out, but kept their distance as the little boy looked up at the pitcher and asked to pitch. Handed the ball, he threw twice in the direction of the home plate.

In the stands, the crowd went wild and gave the boy a standing ovation.

As the man who plays the organ at the ballpark said, "It was like the world stopped for a little while and everybody was able to love a little boy."

The boy's mother scurried out to the mound, apologized to the pitcher and led the little fellow away. But not before he tugged at the pitcher's sleeve and hugged his neck.

Back on the mound, the young pitcher's one-hitter was in big trouble. He began to cry. He walked the next batter on four pitches. The next guy up hit a double. The pitcher kept crying, and had to be taken from the game.

"I was in a groove that night," Gray said later. "At first I thought this isn't happening!...He got to the mound and I saw that he was mentally handicapped and I didn't want to be mean to him...So I handed him the ball. And he promptly threw a strike!"

Gray wondered how his teammates would react.

"We're supposed to be tough and strong. 'Hey kid. Get out of my way...' I had a great game going, but I wouldn't trade that with what happened for anything in the world."

We're told that real, soul-searing tears can be therapeutic, even for men who, these days, can cry occasionally without appearing less manly. Still, for many of us, they usually mark some rare moment in our lives. Such as recalling the death of a little dog or letting a little boy live a moment's glory.

October 1993

It beats priming tobacco

A reader this week wrote regarding the author "O'Henry." Yeah, in my hurry, I copied the error in a letter from one of my fans. I've known since high school that it's O. Henry.

Alas, too late. Elisabeth Bowles, one of my wife's friends and a former professor at UNCG, writes that that seeing O. Henry written as O'Henry is absolutely her greatest peeve in all the world of really great peeves.

Not long before that, in a column on wedding stamps, I failed to mention that the post office has a 52-cent stamp featuring Hubert Humphrey's face. Can you imagine the Happy Warrior's face going out on wedding invitations?

The reader, who was too shy to sign his name, raged: "Why don't you, Dennis Rogers, Lewis Grizzard and others of your kind get a real job anyway?"

Now hold on here, friend. I don't know what you do for a living. And I know that newspapering is easier than digging ditches or spreading asphalt on a 98-degree day. But to put it in plain, ungrammatical language, it ain't no picnic.

Try getting up at 6 a.m. for 35 years and spending your days dealing with deadlines, and with reporters who are the most creative — and often obstreperous (that's a fancy word for boisterously stubborn) — people in the world.

Try fielding telephone calls from subscribers who think (as well they should) that because they buy your product, they also buy your soul. Try scanning the pages after the press run, desperately hoping you haven't misspelled a word or name, because if you have, you'll be verbally drawn and quartered, if not sued for several million.

Lewis Grizzard, in one of his earlier books, said it's amazing that everybody hates the newspaper. Regardless of what town you're in, people are always cussing the newspaper.

"Don't worry about the newspaper," he says. "Let me tell you what you should worry about. Television."

And, he adds, especially television news.

"You know what I hate about television news? Everybody's always so happy on television news. Everybody's chatting on, the weatherman chats over here, and the anchor person chats over there and they are just having a good time. You might not know this. But them folks are 'nekkid' from the waist down. That's why they so happy."

After a column I wrote on the tough life of preachers' kids, I received a delightful anecdote from the Rev. Bob Yandle of Sanford.

His son, Tony, was a second-grader when the teacher one day paused at his desk as he was chewing thoughtfully on his art-gum eraser.

Seizing the opportunity to teach a lesson in frugality, she said sternly, "Tony! Why are you destroying that eraser?"

Tony listened with apprehension as the teacher continued to lecture.

"Tony, my husband must work very hard for everything we have, and if we want anything we must take care of what he provides for us."

Allowing the lesson to sink in, she then added "Didn't your father work hard so he could buy that eraser for you?"

"No, ma'am,' Tony replied. "He just preaches!"

This is the sort of thing my children would have said regarding my profession: "He just writes."

Through the years, when I felt ill-used by my job, I'd always compare it with priming tobacco, and would cheer up pronto. If you don't know what priming tobacco is all about, there is no way I can adequately describe that particular kind of dirty, obnoxious, back-breaking labor.

You have to have experienced it to appreciate it. As a friend said recently, "When people talk about running around like a chicken with its head cut off, I know what they're talking about. Because I've seen a chicken with its head cut off."

I remember something Chicago columnist Bob Greene said many years ago:

"The business I am in is a strange one. I intrude into people's lives for an hour or a day or a week, and I scrape their lives for what I can, and then I display the scrapings to strangers. I get paid for this: Whether it is a moral calling or not, I do not know, but I have no other craft."

"When you write about people in a personal way, they react strongly. It is as if you have been in bed with them; the experience stays with them, and often you will hear from them years later."

I'm not sure I subscribe to that in its entirety. This job is different. But it's still work, still a "real" job, sometimes very demanding, full of pressures and deadlines. And, as one of our reporters knows from recent experience, it's a job on which you can get shot at.

So, sir, don't tell me I should have gotten a "real job."

Fortunately, for me, I have loved almost every moment of it. And as I said earlier, it sure beats priming tobacco. Or preaching.

October 1993

Mozart in Wolfpack's den

I do not consider myself a connoisseur of culture. But I can fake it as well as the next person, having had years of experience.

Not long ago, I sat in Reynolds Coliseum waiting for the great Isaac Stern to appear on stage. Attending the Friends of the College concert on this particular night had not been my idea, so I was not in a very receptive mood.

"How remarkable!" my wife said, reading the program. "Isaac Stern is going to perform with four major symphonies this year. And he's 72 years old!"

"Ed Green is 81," I said, referring to our much-admired neighbor up the street.

"Yes, I know. But Ed doesn't play the violin."

"No, but he can split a cord of wood, go dancing two nights a week, ride a bike 15 miles, clean out my gutters and install a new valve in an ailing commode in no time flat."

"But playing the violin requires such concentration!"

"So does installing a stubborn commode valve while standing on your head."

Pretty soon, under the maestro's spell, the savage breast within me was soothed.

I closed my eyes, forgot I was in a basketball arena, shut out the sight of bright red Wolfpack ceiling pennants proclaiming Dixie Classic and ACC championships, and closed my ears to the rumble of the nightly freight train crossing the campus in the middle of the Mozart sonata.

I found myself thinking about "Miss Martha," and feeling guilty about my earlier lack of enthusiasm for Stern's genius.

I have the late Miss Martha Biggers to thank for whatever appreciation for classical music I do have.

A tall, sweet-faced woman of uncommon serenity, "Miss Martha" was head of the music department at the small junior college I attended after returning from the South Pacific at the end of World War II.

On the way to the class, my path took me past "Miss Martha's" second-floor studio in the Music Building.

"I looked out the window and saw you, and God said, 'Pay attention to that young man,'" she told me later. "Miss Martha" was one of the first saints I ever knew close up.

Pretty soon, I was listening to Beethoven concertos, boning up on the plots of great operas and going to Civic Music concerts in Asheville.

She made no silk purse from the sow's ear God sent her. But now, when listening to a symphony, I do know enough not to applaud at the end of a movement, which is more than I can say for several hundred others at Mr. Stern's performance.

In Willa Cather's short story, "A Wagner Matinee," the young Clark tells about his Aunt Georgiana, a Boston musician and piano teacher who married a young farmer and moved to the desolate, dreary outback of a Nebraska farm.

During 33 years of bleak existence, the woman was cut off almost entirely from music. Late in life, she took a train East to claim a modest inheritance. Her husband had written Clark, asking him to look after her during her brief visit.

One night, he took her to the opera. After the cascade of soaring sound from Siegfried's funeral march had faded, Aunt Georgiana sat in her seat, weeping. Even after the hall emptied and the musician had left the stage, she still sat there.

"I don't want to go, Clark! I don't want to go," she moaned piteously.

The nephew understood.

"For her, just outside the door of the concert hall lay the black pond with the cattle-tracked bluffs; the tall, unpainted house with weather-curled boards, naked as a tower; the crook-backed ash seedlings where the dish-cloths hung to dry; the gaunt, moulting turkeys picking up refuse about the kitchen door."

Whatever its form, great music steals us away from the wasteland of life. It cracks the door to the soul, letting in the light that enables us to return to the ordinary, convinced that it's not really ordinary.

January 1994

Time's little ticking moments

I was re-reading Thomas Wolfe's "You Can't Go Home Again" when the mail brought the advance booklet for the Class of 1954's reunion at Woman's College (now UNC-G).

I started thumbing through the brief autobiographies of the group of women who graduated amid daisy chains, Saturday night cries of "Man on the hall!" and high heels and hats on Sunday. The in-state charge for tuition, room and board was $585, compared to today's $4,767.

On a recent trip to the beach with a "WC" grad at the wheel, I continued perusing the thumbnail sketches of four decades of living.

"Are you sure this is the class of '54?" I asked, as my eyes roved over one graduate's offering. "It reads more like Class of '94!"

"What do you mean?"

"Listen to this. 'Today my life is full of fun: aerobics, windsurfing, biking, tennis and skiing,. My family consists of three kitties and a 'sweetie, a POSSLQ, who agrees with me that we don't want to spoil our beautiful relationship with marriage. I wish I had those 40 years to live over!"

"Good heavens!" said my wife. "Well, Mary Ann was always a bit unusual. She expected a lot out of life."

"Sounds as if she got it, too."

I'd like this woman, I thought, as I read one piece, which opened with "I am a survivor! To God be the glory!"

She had survived a number of obstacles, including her own bout with cancer and the loss of her husband to the same disease.

"I said he wouldn't die. He did," she wrote. I sensed her sadness, tinged with bitterness. "Remember how the Tobacco Road representatives used to pass out cigarettes in the dorms?"

"Uh-oh," I said. "Here's another one of the 'girls' who has lost her husband. She now has a 'steady fellow' and they enjoy sailing, traveling and cooking together. Is that the sort of thing you plan to do when I pass on?"

"Wilbur's is just ahead. Do you think we ought to stop there for lunch or just keep going?" she replied, ignoring the question.

Class of '54 accomplished much more than I would have guessed. Even in 1954, women were still treated as second class citizens, including being denied admission to the elitist Chapel Hill branch unless they were pharmacy or grad students.

Although more became teachers than anything else, the roster of graduates included lawyers, bankers, chemists, social workers, successful artists. One became a director of the NBC radio network. Another spent years in the foreign service.

Perhaps there is truth to the claim that all-women campuses better prepare women for leadership roles, independence, and rich, full lives that extend far beyond changing diapers and playing bridge at the club.

"What was Gertrude like?" I asked, after reading one woman's impressive list of accomplishments.

"Oh, Gertie B. was pretty, petite and bright. As Amanda Wingfield would say, she had lots of charm and vivacity. Why do you ask?"

"Well, where the questionnaire asked 'Husband?' she has written 'He ran away from home sometime during the past two decades.'"

"All I can say is that a man would have to be out of his mind to leave Gertie B," my wife said with conviction.

After a few moments of silence, I muttered to myself, "Yeah, I'll bet."

"What did you say?"

"One of your classmates says her son, who is manager of a box plant, 'has funny stories to tell about golf and Clinton.' I know the type. Well, I guess he's getting a lot of new material these days for his 'funny' stories about Clinton."

"My most exciting news is that I am now engaged to Jack Claiborne, my sweetheart during most of my years in high school and at W.C.," noted Barbara Jean, who husband had died. "We had not seen each other in 36 years until our 40th high school reunion brought us together."

Thomas Wolfe is wrong. You can go home again. The Class of '54 did just that, coming from far and near.

Nevertheless, at every reunion for those past 50, amid the hugs and cries of joy and excitement, there lurk haunting memories of those whose names are listed on the "In Memoriam" page. One of my wife's roommates has died; another has been widowed twice.

Betty Ann said it for all the surviving members of Class of '54: "I wonder how long we have left...time passes."

It brought to my mind Wolfe's sorrowful line in "Of Time and the River." He refers to time as "dark delicate time, the little ticking moments of strange time count us into death. Now in the dark, I hear the passing of dark time."

But for a fleeting weekend, they are together again, young again and for one shining moment, immortal again.

May 1994

Toast the coach's 'lovely wife'

During the March madness now in full sway and the April mayhem that lies ahead, you'll see her there, sitting just behind the coach's bench, dressed in the school colors, waving her pompom, biting her nails, and, at game's end, leaping to her feet in ecstasy or weeping into her Kleenex in despair.

From time to time the TV's all-seeing eye will pause at her place, and the sportscaster will murmur condescendingly, "And there's the coach's lovely wife."

Although I may be pulling against their teams, I feel compassion for these women. No matter the game's outcome, they have to go home with the coach. Imagine, if you can, what going home with Bobby Knight is like after losing to Minnesota by 50 points!

Recently, a New York publishing house publicist invited me to a Triangle luncheon and press conference for Terry Phelps, whose husband, Notre Dame coach Digger Phelps, was forced out of his job a couple of seasons ago.

Digger only produced 18 of 20 winning seasons and saw every one of his players graduate. That's right — a 100 percent graduation rate!

Over the years, I seldom pulled for Notre Dame. For good reason. The Irish whomped the Tar Heels in football 13 of 14 times. But somehow I've always liked Digger Phelps' clean-cut appearance and almost boyish enthusiasm for basketball and for life itself.

I also liked his commitment to academics. A player who skipped even one class knew he'd be riding the bench during the next game.

Coaches, especially jilted ones, are always coming out with books. Coaches' wives seldom have their say.

But what wife doesn't have a story to tell? Wives are the human blotters who absorb the anger, grief and pain that every husband brings home, whether he is coach, plumber, farmer, candlestick maker or newspaperman.

I couldn't make the press conference. But when a copy of "The Coach's Wife" arrived in the mail, I was pleasantly surprised.

Terry Phelps' well-written story is no ordinary "somebody done somebody wrong" song.

For one thing, Terry Phelps strips away some of the magic and mystique long associated with Notre Dame, revealing the clay feet and human frailties common to almost every big-time sports program.

The deep chill set in as soon as a new priest replaced Father Theodore Hesburgh, (cq) a longtime believer that sports should play second fiddle to academics.

"The Coach's Wife" also is the account of an intelligent, strong-willed and articulate woman seeking her own identity, firmly refuting the idea that sports are the end-all of life.

The book has its light moments. Constantly striving to teach her children to keep the game in perspective, Mrs. Phelps once feared she had overdone the job.

During a nail-biting game with Kentucky for the No. 1 national ranking, Notre Dame trailed by one point with 30 seconds left. Son Rick, 10, seated just behind the bench, reached over and tapped Digger on the shoulder: "Dad, could I have a quarter for a Coke?"

Strange as it seems, Coach Phelps' crime may have been succeeding too dramatically at a school where, since the Knute Rockne days, football has competed with Catholicism as the school's religion.

In a Thursday night National Invitational Tournament game against Fordham in Madison Square Garden, the basketball team performed without the Notre Dame band in attendance. But the strains of the school's famous fight song could be heard from a distance as the band practiced nearby in preparation for the football team's game with Penn on Saturday.

In addition to raising three children and nurturing her husband during 20 years of hazardous duty as a college coach, Mrs. Phelps earned three degrees at Notre Dame and is a member of its law faculty.

Imagine anyone, much less a coach's wife, introducing the nuances of "The Love Song of J. Alfred Prufrock" to a classroom of fledgling legal eagles!

In spite of the trauma surrounding her husband's departure, Terry Phelps still loves the place.

Notre Dame, she says, "made me a person who could talk about the soul without being embarrassed."

In the same vein, her sportscaster husband shouldn't be embarrassed if he slips up occasionally and mentions on the tube that Notre Dame probably won't qualify for this year's NCAA tournament.

March 1994

The right to remain naked

The Charlotte Hornets star Alonzo Mourning got into hot water recently for supposedly cursing a a female sports writer who refused to leave the locker room.

Alonzo wanted to get out of his sweat clothes and into something comfortable but he didn't want to do it in front of a woman.

So when the Atlanta-Constitution reporter refused to leave, he became verbal.

Now there's a problem that I thought had gone away. But apparently it hasn't. And I suppose never will.

There will always be men who, like Adam in the Garden of Eden, want a little privacy, even if it's only a fig leaf. Especially in front of strange women.

Even today's youngsters, who know more sex at 16 than adults used to know at 60, are puzzled by today's invasion of men's dressing rooms by women reporters.

One of the first questions put to me during a seminar for high school seniors at Peace College last spring was: "Why should female sports writers be allowed in male athletes' dressing rooms?"

This problem is peculiar to sports alone. No reporters, male or female, insist on the right to interview Agriculture Commissioner Jim Graham as he sits in the YMCA steam room trying to take off a few pounds.

Nobody is asking the Big Jim about next year's sweet potato acreage or pinning him down on his position on President Clinton's proposed cigarette tax while he's behind a towel.

Nor does anyone confront Governor Jim Hunt for a comment on North Carolina's SAT score increase as he steps out of the shower after rinsing off the sweat and grime of a hard day's duty on his Eagle Rock cattle farm.

I, myself, have been interviewed a number of times over the years, but, God forbid, not once in the nude. Not even in a bathrobe.

As my friend and former preacher, Dr. Albert Edwards once said from the pulpit, "God made nothing uglier than a man without clothes on."

Veteran sports writer Bruce Phillips chuckles over an episode that occurred years ago when a Fayetteville Observer reporter, one of the first women to come near a men's locker room, was covering a game at Reynolds Coliseum.

The young woman and Bruce were standing side by side waiting for the coach to show. A player whose name became a household word when N.C. State won its last national championship came out of the shower and started down the hall to the dressing room.

As the young man strode past, buck naked, one of the male reporters murmured, "Hmmm."

"I didn't see it! I didn't see it!" the young woman replied, turning away and blushing mightily.

As I told the high schoolers, contrary to the stereotype of the male as a totally insensitive soul, the average man is basically shy, and is not an exhibitionist.

He treasures his privacy as much as the average woman treasures her—especially in the presence of strangers of the opposite sex.

Still there is a paradox here. Although we have gone to great lengths, and rightly so, to provide equal access for female writers to the men's locker room, the walls of sexual discrimination still stand impenetrable where women's sports are concerned.

I have not heard of any male reporters walking in on members of UNC or N.C. State's women's basketball or soccer teams as they emerge from the showers.

I once interviewed Evangeline Davis, one of the South's if not the country's first woman sports writer.

Ms. Davis, once the number one tennis player in the South, was hired as a sports writer on the Atlanta Constitution by Ralph McGill, perhaps the Constitution's greatest editor. She never went near a locker room.

Neither she nor I, of course, think that women who demand access to locker rooms are closet peeping Janes. They just want to do their jobs on equal footing with their male counterparts, who have long been welcome in the showers.

The solution is so easy and painless I wonder what all the hullabaloo is about. Provide a room where only clothed athletes of either sex are interviewed—either before or after their showers—by both male and female members of the press.

In that way, no one can question female reporters' professional objectivity. And no one will feel deprived of equal rights to an interview.

October 1990

Four drinks, you're a pig

A fellow by the name of Henry Volliam Martin at the turn of the century wrote "One drink of wine, and you act like a monkey; two drinks and you strut like a peacock; three drinks, and you roar like a lion; and four drinks — you behave like a pig."

The quote came to mind recently as, walking down Fayetteville Street Mall, I almost stumbled over a man and a woman sitting on the ledge of a flower bed. A spent wine bottle lay nearby.

"I thought you loved me," she wailed loudly, explaining in explicit street language, how he had had sex with her the previous night "and left me laying in the bushes like common trash."

He endured the vocal abuse in sullen silence for several minutes before exploding.

"Trash!" he bellowed. "That's exactly what you are, woman. Common trash!"

I walked on down the mall, out of range of their fury and frustration. The previous week, in Penzance, England, as we were about to board the overnight sleeper for London, I met my first Welshman. He was half-drunk, but still somewhat charming.

After introducing himself, he laid an arm over my wife's shoulder and mine and said thickly, "Surely, before our train leaves, ye have time to have a drink with me."

"'Tis true, I'm a wee bit drunk already. In fact, I may be a wee bit more than a wee bit drunk, but I mean no harm. Me wife tells me I can't come home drunk, which makes no sense to me because a man a wee bit drunk is better than no man at all, wouldn't ye say?"

I allowed as how he was probably right. My wife wasn't so sure.

"But she's a good woman is me wife," he said. "We been together close on 30 years. I go home. We go to bed. Sometimes we do a little biz; sometimes we don't do a little biz. But we get along."

He had been in the Royal Navy. It seems all the men in England have been in the Royal Navy at one time or another. And he was full of talk about Yanks. "All mouth and trousers," he said, with a wink. "But they saved us in the war, ye know. And we're grateful."

"We're a drinking breed," he said. "Ye know of our poet, Dylan Thomas. Good verses, heavy drinking."

He pointed out over the bay and said "That's where the queen comes on her yacht. She never bothers with us commoners. But Prince Charlie, now there's a lad for ye."

"Isn't he the one who was stepping out on his wife?"

"Oh, now, sir, don't fault the lad for that. A man needs experience.

He's our prince, ye know — the Prince of Wales. He's an all right lad."

As we boarded the sleeping car, the Welshman reluctantly bade us farewell and walked slowly down the track to board a coach that would take him to his waiting wife a town or two up the line.

A few days after our encounter with the Welshman I read that the wife of Dylan Thomas had died.

Caitlin Thomas once described her marriage to Dylan as "raw, red, bleeding meat."

Dylan Thomas died in New York four decades ago, after a night of heavy drinking in Greenwich Village. At the hospital, his estranged wife burst into the room where Thomas was attended by his mistress.

"Is the bloody man dead yet?" she screamed in a rage, bit an attendant and fought with bystanders who tried to subdue her.

While in England, I re-read Thomas Hardy's classic, "The Mayor of Casterbridge" in which Michael Hencherd, the hero, as a young man takes his wife and baby to the Casterbridge fair.

While there, he gets to drinking and ends up auctioning off his wife to a passing sailor.

Now you may shudder at such an outrageously foul deed but as someone, a woman, in fact, remarked upon hearing the story, "What husband at one time or another has not considered doing the same thing?"

Anyway, Hencherd, taking a vow to lay off the liquor for 20 years, goes on to become a successful merchant and mayor of Casterbridge. His life is incredibly complicated by the return of his wife and daughter 20 years later.

Basically, Hencherd was a good man all his life, but that one drunken hour cost him his happiness in the end.

Not every drunk is as entertaining as the Welshman in Penzance or as repentant as the mayor of Casterbridge.

As Charlie Chaplin once said, after the drunken Dylan Thomas had embarrassed him at a party given by Chaplin in the poet's honor, "Even great poetry cannot excuse such rude, drunken behavior."

This piece is not intended as a temperance lecture, but to point out that each person handles his demons differently. One man gets drunk and goes home and writes a poem; another, in a similar condition, goes home and beats his wife.

Or sells her at public auction.

August 1994

Going home

The imposing, slate-rock two-story house sits far back from the highway, surrounded by a grove of mighty oaks. I make the turn into the driveway as swiftly as possible, hoping she will not notice the "For Sale" sign on the front lawn.

I park the car near the back steps. Even with the walker, it is an effort for her to put one foot before the other.

She sits there for a long moment, drinking it all in, whispering softly, "I can't believe it! I just can't believe it!"

She is a proud woman, on her own for more than 40 years after her young, energetic husband died of a heart attack at 42. I turn away, not wanting her to know I have noticed the tears coursing down her cheeks.

Once inside the house, she pauses in the back hall, turning to whisper, "Thank you! Oh, thank you!"

She has never been one to over-thank her children. She has devoted her life to helping others to the extent that doing for loved ones is taken for granted. But that is not the case today. Her gratitude is overwhelming.

She moves down the hall slowly, like a frail shadow. She glances into the den where she spent most of her time before we took her away to the retirement center in Raleigh.

Through these windows, over the years, she viewed her flower beds, the sweep of fields, the flame azalea she had transplanted from a mountain trip with us when she was younger, prettier and actually vivacious.

She had persuaded the plant to grow in the hot Piedmont, where the experts said it could not grow. She has always had a green thumb.

"So pretty, so pretty," she murmurs, glancing about the rooms, not noticing, at least not mentioning, a few absent items and the family portraits missing from the den wall.

I follow her into the living room, from where she so often watched the most splendid sunsets I have ever shared.

I never understood why, across the open fields and a busy highway, the sun's daily departure was staged with such spectacular splendor. It was as if God did it just for her, perhaps in atonement for her long years of loneliness, her uncomplaining endurance.

In the dining room, she glides her small hand across the glossy surface of the mahogany table that has held so many feasts for so many people. The lucky diners had included not only her children and grandchildren, her in-laws and other relatives.

Decades ago, they included the wheat threshers and tobacco primers in a time when farm hands and neighbors were almost willing to work only for the opportunity to slide their feet under the table at "the rock house," as it was known in the community.

I sit with her at the table, my mind churning with the nostalgia of happy times that I, her son-in-law, have shared in this place. I almost hear the happy chatter of women as they moved the steaming dishes of food from kitchen to dining room.

The walls echo the exasperated cries of "You men turn off that football game and get in here before this food gets cold!"

The meals were endless orgies of goodness. After the pecan pie, and occasionally the persimmon pudding that only she could make to perfection, we would linger with our coffee and conversation, while her grandchildren romped through the house or, impatiently shaking the gifts under the Christmas tree, whined "Let's open the presents. Now!"

Eventually, often after midnight, we would climb the stairs to the bedrooms. My wife and I slept in the "room over the garage," unheated for the most part, snuggling under the warm homemade quilts, lulled to sleep by the ceaseless flow of traffic racing past on Highway 311.

Sometimes, before we drifted off completely, a small, ghostlike figure in a nightgown would steal into the room, spread an additional blanket or quilt at the foot of the bed.

"Good night, again," a voice would whisper.

In the morning, we would race barefoot down the stairs to the living room and the roaring fire. There we would linger over the first cup of coffee, basking before the blaze and then moving across the hall to the dining room and homemade waffles, bacon, eggs and fruit. And, of course, more conversation.

Today, as I stand in the upstairs bedroom and look out the window at the world she has loved for more than half a century, I can well understand the emotions tearing at the heart of the woman downstairs. After 35 years in the family, I, too, feel an almost stifling sadness at leaving this place.

A victim of Alzheimer's, she has come home, probably for the last time, to embrace the house she has asked to see for the past nine months. She has come home to say, forever, goodbye to the house that has held her, her husband, her children, her memories — her life.

After a few hours, she says quietly, "I know I can't stay. I guess we might as well go."

Luck was not with us as we drove down the driveway toward the highway. A heavy surge of traffic delayed us long enough for her to spot the offensive sign.

"Oh, is that a 'For Sale' sign?" she asks, almost in a whisper.

I try to explain away, actually lie away, the painful truth by saying it has to do with an adjacent strip of land that is being sold.

She may or may not have believed me. Anyway, she was never one to complain, accepting what came her way with grace and dignity.

Next day, she does not, of course, remember the trip, still asking to return one more time to her once-happy world.

I tell her that we have just been there. I tell her what a good time we had and how pleased she was to be there.

And she says, "Thank you. I'm glad you told me. I'm glad I've been."

And then she asks, "Was it the same?"

And I say, "Oh yes, the same."

For it was, at the moment.